Information Literacy in the Digital Age

CHANDOS
INFORMATION PROFESSIONAL SERIES

Series Editor: Ruth Rikowski
(email: Rikowskigr@aol.com)

Chandos' new series of books is aimed at the busy information professional. They have been specially commissioned to provide the reader with an authoritative view of current thinking. They are designed to provide easy-to-read and (most importantly) practical coverage of topics that are of interest to librarians and other information professionals. If you would like a full listing of current and forthcoming titles, please visit www.chandospublishing.com or email wp@woodheadpublishing.com or telephone +44 (0) 1223 499140.

New authors: we are always pleased to receive ideas for new titles; if you would like to write a book for Chandos, please contact Dr Glyn Jones on email gjones@chandospublishing.com or telephone number +44 (0) 1993 848726.

Bulk orders: some organisations buy a number of copies of our books. If you are interested in doing this, we would be pleased to discuss a discount. Please email wp@woodheadpublishing.com or telephone +44 (0) 1223 499140.

Information Literacy in the Digital Age

An evidence-based approach

TERESA S. WELSH
AND
MELISSA S. WRIGHT

CP
CHANDOS
PUBLISHING

Oxford Cambridge New Delhi

Chandos Publishing
Hexagon House
Avenue 4
Station Lane
Witney
Oxford OX28 4BN
UK
Tel: +44 (0) 1993 848726
Email: info@chandospublishing.com
www.chandospublishing.com

Chandos Publishing is an imprint of Woodhead Publishing Limited

Woodhead Publishing Limited
80 High Street
Sawston
Cambridge CB22 3HJ
UK
Tel: +44 (0) 1223 499140
Fax: +44 (0) 1223 832819
www.woodheadpublishing.com

First published in 2010

ISBN: 978-1-84334-515-2 (print)
ISBN: 978-1-78063-035-9 (online)

© T.S. Welsh and M.S. Wright, 2010

British Library Cataloguing-in-Publication Data.
A catalogue record for this book is available from the British Library.

Typeset by Domex e-Data Pvt. Ltd.
Printed in the UK and USA.

Printed in the UK by 4edge Limited - www.4edge.co.uk

To our many students in LIS 201, Introduction to Information Literacy, who inspired us to write this book.

To Janet Boswell, Sharon Davis, Lajuan Davis-Bisnette, Glenda Ford, Lilian Hill, Linda Matthews, Rodney Marshall, and John Rachal for allowing us to use their materials. Your contributions made this a much stronger book. (*TSW and MSW*)

To my mother, Martha Wright, for always encouraging me to press on. (*MSW*)

To my parents, Tercy and Mary Smith, for instilling me with a love of learning and to my best friend and husband, Bud, for his love and support. (*TSW*)

Contents

List of figures and tables

Figures

Tables

List of abbreviations

AASL	American Association of School Librarians
ACRL	Association of College and Research Libraries
AHIP	Academy of Health Information Professionals
ALA	American Library Association
ARPA	Advanced Research Projects Agency
BAC	British Accreditation Council
CAP	California Achievement Program
CIBER	Centre for Information Behaviour and Evaluation of Research
CILIP	Chartered Institute of Library and Information Professionals
CLRIT	Commission on Learning Resources and Instructional Technology
CMC	computer-mediated communication
CPU	central processing unit
CSAP	Colorado Student Assessment Program
CSU	California State University
CTEA	Copyright Term Extension Act 1998 (US)
DARPA	Defense Advanced Research Projects Agency
DDS	Dewey Decimal System
DIKW	date, information, knowledge, wisdom
DNS	domain name system
DoD	Department of Defense
ENIAC	Electronic Numerical Integrator and Computer
ERIC	Educational Resources Information Center
FICO	Fair Isaac Corporation
FTP	File Transmission Protocol
GIS	geographic information system
HTML	Hypertext Markup Language
IANA	Internet Assigned Numbers Authority
IBM	International Business Machines
ICANN	Internet Corporation for Assigned Names and Numbers

ICT	information and communication technologies
IFLA	International Federation of Library Associations and Institutions
IHL	institution of higher learning
IL	information literacy
IMD	Internet Movie Database
IMLS	Institute of Museum and Library Services
ISP	Internet service provider
ITBS	Iowa Test of Basic Skills
JELIS	*Journal of Education for Library and Information Science*
LARC	Livermore Atomic Research Computer
LC	Library of Congress
LIS	library and information science
LISA	Library and Information Science Abstracts
LISTA	Library, Information Science & Technology Extracts
LMC	library media center
LMS	Libraries and Media Services (Kent State University, Ohio)
MAP	Missouri Assessment Program
MCAS	Massachusetts Comprehensive Assessment System
MDE	Mississippi Department of Education
MEAP	Michigan Educational Assessment Program
MLA	Medical Library Association
MSM	mainstream media
NARA	US National Archives and Records Administration
NCATE	National Council of Accreditation for Teacher Education
NCLIS	National Commission on Libraries and Information Science
NCSA	National Center for Supercomputing Applications
NCTE	National Council of Teachers of English
NMAAP	New Mexico Achievement Assessment Program
NSF	National Science Foundation
OASIS	Online Advancement of Student Information Skills
ODLIS	*Online Dictionary of Library and Information Science*
OED	*Oxford English Dictionary*
OPAC	online public access catalog
PBS	Public Broadcasting Service
PC	personal computer
PSSA	Pennsylvania System of School Assessment
RAE	Research Assessment Exercise (UK)
RAM	random-access memory

RDF	Resource Description Framework
ROM	read-only memory
SACS	Southern Association of Colleges and Schools (US)
SAILS	Standardized Assessment of Information Literacy Sklls
SCANS	Secretary's Commission on Achieving Necessary Skills
SuDoc	Superintendent of Documents
TAAS	Texas Assessment of Academic Skills
TC/IP	Transmission Control Protocol/Internet Protocol
TLD	top-level domain
TRAILS	Tool for Real-time Assessment of Information Literacy Skills
UGC	user-generated content
UKOLN	UK Office of Libraries and Networking
UNIVAC	Universal Automatic Computer
URL	uniform/universal resource locator
W3C	World Wide Web Consortium
XML	Extensible Markup Language

About the authors

Teresa S. Welsh is an Associate Professor at the University of Southern Mississippi School of Library and Information Science. Areas of interest include visualization of information, distance education, archival studies, knowledge management, information literacy, and research methodologies. She has a Bachelor of Arts degree in anthropology from the University of Southern Mississippi, a Master of Library and Information Science degree from the University of Tennessee, and a PhD in Communications and Information, with a primary concentration in Information Sciences, from the University of Tennessee.

Melissa S. Wright is a doctoral candidate in adult education at the University of Southern Mississippi. She is also an instructional services librarian at Rowland Medical Library at the University of Mississippi. Areas of interest include adult education, the education of adults with disabilities, international adult education, public libraries, reference, children's literature, young adult literature, and storytelling. She has a Bachelor of Arts degree in French and Spanish from Mississippi College, Masters of Arts degrees in English and applied linguistics from Mississippi State University and Indiana University respectively, and a Master of Library and Information Science degree from the University of Southern Mississippi.

The authors may be contacted via the publishers.

What is information literacy?

The purpose of this opening chapter is to gain a better understanding of the term 'information literacy' by examining its origins, some definitions, and some models or standards of information literacy. This first chapter thus serves as a foundation for an *evidence-based* approach to teaching information literacy.

To understand the concept of information literacy, it is useful to begin by knowing the origin and literal meaning of the terms. The word *information* is from the Latin *informatio*, meaning concept or idea. The word *literate* is from the Latin *literatus*, meaning learned or lettered.

Over time, the definition of information literacy has changed. The traditional definition of literacy was the ability to read and write at a basic level and sign a document. More recently, the United States Workforce Investment Act of 1998[1] defined literacy as 'an individual's ability to read, write, speak in English, compute, and solve problems at levels of proficiency necessary to function on the job, in the family of the individual, and in society.' As the world is moving from the information age to the digital age, new definitions of information literacy are evolving that include how to access information in digital formats and how to evaluate information and use it appropriately.

According to the American Library Association (ALA), information literacy is 'increasingly important in the contemporary environment of rapid technological change and proliferating information resources':

- Information literacy is a set of abilities requiring individuals to recognize when information is needed and have the ability to locate, evaluate, and use effectively the needed information.

- Information literacy forms the basis for lifelong learning and is common to *all disciplines*, to *all learning environments*, and to *all levels of education*.[2]

Models of information literacy

To become information literate, one must understand the definition and context of information. One way to understand information and to put it in context is to visualize it as part of the DIKW hierarchy or pyramid: Data, Information, Knowledge, Wisdom (see Figure 1.1[3]).

According to the KIT Institute in the Netherlands:

- *Data* are raw statistics and facts.
- *Information* comprises the basic facts with context and perspective.
- *Knowledge* is information which provides guidance for action.
- *Wisdom* is understanding which knowledge to use for what purpose.[4]

The DIKW hierarchy puts the concept of information into context. That is, there must be an understanding of data or facts for those data to become information and some understanding of information patterns for information to become knowledge.

According to Cleveland,[5] the origin of the DIKW hierarchy is a poem by T.S. Eliot in 1934 entitled 'The Rock':

> *Where is the Life we have lost in living?*
> *Where is the wisdom we have lost in knowledge?*
> *Where is the knowledge we have lost in information?*[6]

Practical models

The Association of College and Research Libraries (ACRL) defines an information literate individual as one possessing particular skill sets and who is able to:

Figure 1.1 Conceptual model: DIKW hierarchy

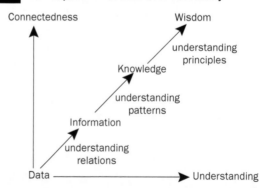

- *determine* the extent of information needed;
- *access* the needed information effectively and efficiently;
- *evaluate* information and its sources critically;
- *incorporate* selected information into one's knowledge base;
- *use* information effectively to accomplish a specific purpose;
- *understand* the economic, legal, and social issues surrounding the use of information, and access and use information ethically and legally.[7]

Information literacy may be considered a *new liberal art*

> ... that extends from knowing how to use computers and access information to critical reflection on the nature of information itself, its technical infrastructure, and its social, cultural and even philosophical context and impact – as essential to the mental framework of the educated information-age citizen as the trivium of basic liberal arts (grammar, logic and rhetoric) was to the educated person in medieval society.[8]

The National Council of Teachers of English (NCTE) maintains that as society and technology changes, the standards of information literacy change. According to NCTE, 'because technology has increased the intensity and complexity of literate environments, the twenty-first century demands that a literate person possess a wide range of abilities and competencies, many literacies.'[9]

The literacies listed by NCTE include the ability to:

- *develop* proficiency with the tools of technology;
- *build* relationships with others to pose and solve problems collaboratively and cross-culturally;
- *design* and share information for global communities to meet a variety of purposes;
- *manage, analyze,* and *synthesize* multiple streams of simultaneous information;
- *create, critique, analyze,* and *evaluate* multimedia texts;
- *attend to the ethical responsibilities* required by these complex environments.[10]

In a similar model, the California Commission on Learning Resources breaks down information literacy as a fusion or integration of several discrete components that will be addressed in this text: *library literacy, computer literacy, media literacy, technological literacy, ethics, critical thinking,* and *communication skills.*[11]

International models

Information literacy is a global concern and effort. The International Federation of Library Associations and Institutions (IFLA) reports on international efforts promoting information literacy by country or region: Australia, Francophone regions, Latin America, Nordic countries, the Russian Federation, Spain, Sub-Saharan Africa, the United Kingdom and the Republic of Ireland, the United States and Canada, and South Africa. The goal of their report, 'Information Literacy: An International State-of-the-Art,'[12] is to identify worldwide trends in information literacy, including: educational resources, information literacy-related publications, information literacy organizations, opportunities for training for information literacy professionals, and conferences and meetings related to information literacy.

The International Information and Communication Technologies (ICT) Literacy Panel has identified four major literacies:

Access:	the ability to retrieve information efficiently and effectively.
Manage/Integrate:	the ability to organize information in a logical and coherent manner and to interpret, summarize, paraphrase, and use information appropriately.
Evaluate:	the ability to access the quality of the information being presented and its relevance to one's needs.
Create:	the ability to create new information based on the appropriate information resources previously retrieved.[13]

The five basic tasks of a virtual scholar identified by UKOLN (UK Office of Libraries and Networking) are:

Discover:	awareness of resources that address a particular information need.
Locate:	ability to find these resources quickly.

Request:	knowledge of the process to obtain the information.
Access:	ability to obtain the full text of the needed information.
Use:	ability to meet one's needs by applying the information retrieved to produce new knowledge.[14]

Information competency

The definitions of information competency typically include competency in accessing information in *electronic* formats.

The Work Group on Information Competence, the Commission on Learning Resources and Instructional Technology (CLRIT), and the California State University (CSU) system define information competence as 'the ability to find, evaluate, use, and communicate information *in all of its various formats.*'[15]

The Secretary's Commission on Achieving Necessary Skills (SCANS) report *What Work Requires of Schools* defines information competence as the ability to: (1) acquire and evaluate information; (2) organize and maintain information; (3) interpret and communicate information; and (4) *use computers* to process information.[16]

What does research indicate about information literacy?

Indications of research on information literacy

The greatest lack of information literacy in teens is in the evaluation of information resources and in the knowledge and use of Boolean operators. The 'Information Literacy Assessment Trial Study of Students in the Eleventh Grade in Mississippi', a 2007 specialist project by Boswell,[17] found that most students scored lowest in these two areas.

Information literacy is a skill set that can be taught. An 'Information Competency Assessment Instrument' (see Appendix 1), developed by Marshall in 2002[18] and used as a pre- and post-test for an undergraduate information literacy course at the University of Southern Mississippi, indicated a measurable improvement in the evaluation of information and information sources.[19]

Research on the Google Generation (defined as those born after 1993) conducted by CIBER (Centre for Information Behaviour and Evaluation of Research at University College London) indicates that while the perception is that teens are very techno-savvy, they tend to be shallow in their information-seeking behaviour:

- Online searching by teens tends to be shallow information-skimming, not in-depth searching.
- Sixty percent visit a site once only and view each web page only for a few seconds.[20]

Librarians are usually the persons who teach information literacy skills and recent studies indicate a positive correlation between having a professional, certified school librarian and student achievement (see Appendix 3).[21]

Indications of research on the virtual scholar

A longitudinal survey of scientists, engineers, and social scientists from 1977 to the present (Tenopir and King, 2000; Tenopir, 2008) indicates that scholars:

- read an increasing number of scholarly articles in not much more time;
- use an increasing number of ways and sources to locate scholarly articles;
- read electronic and print materials;
- read a higher percentage of older articles now than in previous years.[22]

According to Tenopir and King (2000) and Tenopir (2008),[23] the trend for scholarly publishing is granularity – that is, being able to find a particular element of a scholarly article such as a graph of raw data or a particular paragraph of interest. Another trend is that an increasing number of interdisciplinary sources are read by scholars and researchers. Older scholars are more likely to read both print and electronic resources, while younger scholars tend to read more electronic resources.

A study of scholarly activity online by CIBER indicates that access drives use: there is a tremendous use of the scholarly net and about half of the visitors to scholarly websites are robots.

CIBER (Nicholas, 2008) found that human information-seeking behavior tends to be:

- *promiscuous*: 40–50 percent of persons visiting a site do not return;
- *bouncing*: half of website visitors view only 1–3 pages and bounce in and out (scholars bounce less, Google searchers and younger searchers bounce more);
- *flicking*: many users channel hop (a checking form of behavior; some bouncing is attributed to flicking);
- *viewing*: humans do not view an online article longer than 3 minutes, spend more time reading short articles than long ones, or read the abstract and squirrel away the article. Two-thirds of downloads are never read.[24]

Scholarly information-seeking behavior includes power-browsing, where the horizontal replaces the vertical such as scanning three or four books in 15 minutes. Navigation in cyberspace takes up a great deal of time. People spend about half their time viewing content and the other half navigating.[25]

Why is it important to be information literate?

With the rapid technological advances in society today and increased access to said technology by people around the world, becoming information literate is of the utmost importance (see Appendix 4).[26] Globalization, which may be defined as 'a movement of economic integration, of cultural homogenization, and of technological uniformization' (Finger, 2005: 269), is, therefore, a major reason to be information literate.[27] Thus, even though it has been traditionally associated with economics, globalization has become so much more. Brysk (2002) maintains that it is a combination of the following four elements:

- *Connection* – increased amount of interaction and transactions of goods, services, and information from country to country.
- *Cosmopolitanism* – increased number of centers of power and influence worldwide.
- *Communication* – technological advances which have greatly increased international business ventures, economic opportunities, and the transaction of different ideas and values.

- *Commodification* – the expansion of world markets and the increased opportunities to people worldwide.[28]

Thomas Friedman (2005) identifies the following world 'flatteners:' the fall of the Berlin Wall, fiber-optic cable and the 'dot-com' boom, the increase in common software programs and open-source materials, and the increase in the amount of outsourcing by corporations worldwide. He contends that these flatteners 'converged around the year 2000 [to] create a flat world: a global, Web-enabled platform for sharing knowledge and work, irrespective of time, distance, geography, and increasingly, language.'[29] This has greatly increased employment opportunities for people worldwide – people from countries where such opportunities were previously unheard of. Thus if one is not aware of or does not possess the skills to access information quickly, to evaluate this information, and to use this information to create new products and materials, he/she may lose out on valuable economic and social opportunities. To remain competitive in an international market, then, it is imperative to be *information literate*.[30]

Exercises

Exercise 1

1. Before looking below, discuss what you think the following data represent:

   553,988

   269,666

   284,322

   84.7

   32.5

   41,194

2. Now look at the data again with the following additional information provided:

   553,988 – Total population

   269,666 – Total males

   284,322 – Total females

   84.7% – Percent in community possessing at least a high-school education

32.5% – Percent having at least a bachelor's degree

41,194 – Median income

3. Using the knowledge gained from knowing what information the data represent, determine whether or not you would want to live in this community. Why or why not?

Exercise 2

1. Find information on at least three types of automobiles you would like to own.

    ■ What are the three automobiles?

    ■ Which is more economical?

    ■ Which has better gas or petrol mileage?

    ■ Which has the best safety record?

2. Using the information you found above, which car would you buy? Why? Which factors were most important in your buying decision?

Additional sources

Bellinger, Gene, Castro, Durval, and Mills, Anthony (n.d.) 'Data, Information, Knowledge, and Wisdom,' at:
http://www.systems-thinking.org/dikw/dikw.htm.

California State University (n.d.) 'Selected Quotations on Why Information Literacy is Important,' at:
http://www.calstate.edu/LS/InfoQuotes.doc.

Five Colleges of Ohio (n.d.) 'Definitions of Information Literacy and Related Concepts,' at:
http://collaborations.denison.edu/ohio5/grant/about/definitions .html#top.

IFLA InfoLit Global (n.d.) 'Information Literacy Resources Directory,' at:
http://www.infolitglobal.info/.

Notes

1. 'Workforce Investment Act of 1998,' at: *http://www.doleta.gov/regs/statutes/ wialaw.txt* (accessed 15 November 2007).

2. ALA (n.d.) 'Standards,' at: *http://www.ala.org/ala/pio/campaign/sponsorship/ stepuptotheplateyourlibrary/standards.htm* (accessed 12 September 2007).

3. Gene Bellinger, Durval Castro, and Anthony Mills (n.d.) 'Data, Information, Knowledge Wisdom,' at: *http://www.systems-thinking.org/dikw/dikw.htm* (accessed 31 August 2007).

4. KIT Institute (n.d.) 'What Is Knowledge Management?' at: *http://www.kit.nl/ specials/html/km_what_is_knowledge_management.asp?MakeFrame=No&l anguage=* (accessed 26 April 2004).

5. Harland Cleveland (1982) 'Information as resource,' *The Futurist*, December, pp. 34–9.

6. T.S. Eliot (1934) *The Rock*. London: Faber & Faber.

7. ACRL (n.d.) 'Introduction to Information Literacy,' at: *http://www.ala.org/ ala/acrl/acrlissues/acrlinfolit/infolitoverview/introtoinfolit/introinfolit.cfm* (accessed 14 September 2007).

8. Jeremy J. Shapiro and Shelley K. Hughes (1996) 'Information literacy as a liberal art,' *Educom Review*, 3(2), at: *http://www.educause.edu/pub/er/review/ reviewarticles/31231.html* (accessed 12 September 2007).

9. National Council of Teachers of English (2008) 'NCTE's definition of 21st century literacies,' 15 February, at: *http://www.ncte.org/announce/129117 .htm?source=gs* (accessed 1 July 2008).

10. Ibid.

11. California State University (n.d.) 'Information Competencies Final Report,' at: *http://web.archive.org/web/20031028064650/http:/www.calstate.edu/ AcadSen/E-Senator/Reports/ic.shtml* (accessed September 2007).

12. Jesus Lau et al. (2007) 'Information Literacy: An International State-of-the-Art Report,' International Federation of Library Associations (IFLA), Second Draft, May, at: *http://www.infolitglobal.info/docs/UNESCO_IL_ state_of_the_art_report_-_Draft070803.doc* (accessed 24 June 2008).

13. International Information and Communication Technologies (ICT) Literacy Panel (2007) 'Digital Transformation: A Framework for ITC Literacy,' at: *http://www.ets.org/Media/Tests/Information_and_Communication_Technology_ Literacy/ictreport.pdf* (accessed 2 July 2008).

14. Peter Burnhill (2008) 'EDINA and JISC-funded research', *The Virtual Scholar: Second Bloomsbury Conference on E-Publishing and E-Publications*, 26 June.

15. Work Group on Information Competence, Commission on Learning Resources and Instructional Technology (CLRIT), California State University (CSU) System (n.d.) 'Information Competence in the CSU: A Report, December 1995,' at: *http://www.calstate.edu/ls/Archive/info_comp_ report.shtml* (accessed 2 July 2006).

16. Secretary's Commission on Achieving Necessary Skills (SCANS) (1991) *What Work Requires of Schools. A SCANS Report for America 2000*. Washington, DC: Department of Labor, p. 12.

17. Janet Boswell (2007) *Information Literacy Assessment Trial Study of Students in the Eleventh Grade in Mississippi*, Specialist Project, University of Southern Mississippi.

18. Rodney Marshall (2009) 'An instrument to measure information competency,' *Journal of Literacy and Technology: An Academic Journal*, at:

http://www.literacyandtechnology.org/volume7/marshallJLT2006.pdf (accessed 12 October 2009).

19. Sharon Davis and Teresa Welsh (2006) *Development and Evaluation of an Academic Information Literacy Course*. Poster presentation, Mississippi Library Association Annual Meeting, Tunica, MS, 25 October.

20. Ian Rowlands (2008) 'The Google Generation', *The Virtual Scholar: Second Bloomsbury Conference on E-Publishing and E-Publications*, 26 June.

21. Glenda Ford (2009) 'An Examination of the Scholarly Literature Related to School Libraries and Their Impact on Student Achievement,' University of Southern Mississippi, 1 December (see Appendix 3).

22. Carol Tenopir and Donald W. King (2000) *Towards Electronic Journals: Realities for Scientists, Librarians, and Publishers*. Washington, DC: Special Libraries Association; Carol Tenopir (2008) 'The continuing (and not quite complete) transition from print to digital: a long-term view', *The Virtual Scholar: Second Bloomsbury Conference on E-Publishing and E-Publications*, 26 June.

23. Tenopir and King (2000), op. cit.; Tenopir (2008), op. cit.

24. David Nicholas (2008) 'CIBER Research,' *The Virtual Scholar: Second Bloomsbury Conference on E-Publishing and E-Publications*, 26 June.

25. Ibid.

26. Linda Matthews (2009) 'A Bibliometric Analysis of Scholarly Literature Related to Information Literacy and Critical Thinking,' University of Southern Mississippi, 1 December (see Appendix 4).

27. Matthias P. Finger (2005) 'Globalization,' in Leona M. English (ed.), *International Encyclopedia of Adult Education*. New York: Palgrave Macmillan, pp. 269–73.

28. Alison Brysk (2002) *Globalization and Human Rights*. Berkeley, CA: University of California Press.

29. Thomas Friedman (2008) *Flattening the Global Playing Field: Thomas Friedman at the ISB*, Indian School of Business, at: *http://www.isb.edu/media/UsrSiteNewsMgmt.aspx?topicID=305* (accessed 1 September 2008).

30. Thomas Friedman (2005) *The World Is Flat: A Brief History of the Twenty-First Century*. New York: Farrar, Straus & Giroux.

2

Cultural literacy

We have ignored cultural literacy in thinking about education ...
Cultural literacy is the oxygen of social intercourse. (E.D. Hirsch)[1]

What is culture?

The word 'culture' is from the Latin word *cultura*, which means
'cultivation.'

Culture is defined by the *Geography Glossary* (1999)[2] as 'the
accumulated habits, attitudes, and beliefs of a group of people that
define for them their general behavior and way of life; the total set of
learned activities of a people.'

The US National Park Service defines culture as an archaeological
term: '*Common beliefs and practices of a group of people* ... the
integrated pattern of human knowledge, belief, and behavior that
depends upon man's capacity for learning and transmitting knowledge to
succeeding generations.'[3]

Why is cultural literacy important?

Understanding both one's own and other cultures can help a person:

- relate to their surroundings;
- relate to their own culture;
- relate to other cultures;
- gain a broader worldview.

Cultures, while founded upon a set of basic ideas and shared history and
heritage, are constantly changing and evolving. To make things more

complicated, subcultures arise within main cultures. Keeping up with all the cultures and subcultures in the world is a monumental task, and nearly impossible for an individual to do. It is more realistic to focus on learning the basic traits of large, main cultures and then research for more detail on specific cultures or subcultures as one's worldview broadens.

How does one become culturally literate?

Cognitive scientists use the term 'schemas' to describe the mental units into which humans organize knowledge. According to Hirsch's interpretation of schema theory,[4] as humans gain knowledge, they create new schemas and connect them to pre-existing schemas.

Shared knowledge or schemas play an important role in cultural literacy and there are several ways one can increase cultural literacy:

- keep track of current events – local, national, and global;
- be aware of the current trends in technology, entertainment, and literature;
- take the time to read or research about cultures with which one is unfamiliar.

Given the importance of global literacy in a technology-driven world, Robert Rosen, CEO of Healthy Companies International in Washington and the author of *Global Literacies: Lessons on Business Leadership and National Cultures* (2000),[5] recommends the following:

- Use technology in globally literate ways. In a global marketplace, technology is the medium through which people conduct business. While technology accelerates and expands the pace and range of communication, it also increases the chances for miscommunication. Especially with technology through which you can't pick up on physical or emotional cues, you must read between the lines and listen deeply for the emotion, tone, context, and cultural nuances in every communication.
- Learn from the best around the world. Each part of the world excels in a different literacy area. Some Asian cultures, for example, teach us about personal literacy through their ability to understand paradox and ambiguity. Latin American cultures teach us about social literacy by modeling how to build relationships in less organized, constantly changing environments. From European cultures, we learn cultural literacy based on centuries of working and living cross-culturally.

In North America, we learn business literacy by building change-ready, technology-savvy, high-performance organizations in a results-oriented culture.

■ Use culture as a tool for business success. It's vital to understand how your culture influences how you relate to technology. Americans love new technology; they like quick action and excel at creating new things. They tend to abandon ideas that don't show a rapid return on investment. Other cultures react differently. The Japanese, for example, have been more comfortable with incremental improvements.

According to Rubin, adopting these strategies can start one on a path to global literacy. It is a long-term process, and the choice is up to the individual: one can choose to get started, or choose to be left behind.

How can one increase awareness of one's own history and culture?

Many believe that cultural literacy begins with an awareness of one's own history and culture. For instance, it is useful to know the history and culture related to family ancestry:

■ The Church of Jesus Christ of Latter-Day Saints has an extensive collection of genealogy records from around the world. These records are accessible online through their *FamilySearch.org* website.

■ *CensusFinder.com* is a web portal to census information in the United States, United Kingdom, and Canada as well as Native American sources.

One unique way to discover one's ancestry is to find one's origins through DNA testing:

■ The Genographic Project by National Geographic maps individual deep origins through DNA testing. For a fee, a DNA test kit will be sent, the DNA analyzed, and a map tracing a person's ancient origins will be returned. As more people participate in this global project, the human genetic journey will be more fully mapped and understood (*https://genographic.nationalgeographic.com/genographic/index.html*).

■ Genetic Genealogy also uses DNA testing to trace one's deep ancestral roots (*http://www.dnaancestryproject.com/*).

■ *AfricanAncestry.com* is a DNA-testing project for those with African roots.

To understand an individual's context within the world, it is useful to be knowledgeable about the geographic places of origin – one's own state, province, region, and country:

- For information about each of the 50 states in the United States, visit the History Channel website, *The States* (*http://www.history.com/states.do*).
- The BBC has a useful profile on the United Kingdom as well as other countries (*http://news.bbc.co.uk/2/hi/europe/country_profiles/1038758.stm*).
- The *CIA World Factbook* (*https://www.cia.gov/library/publications/the-world-factbook/countrylisting.html*) is a good resource for geographic and statistical information for each country.

After learning about one's own geographic location, it is useful to research other places of interest. According to William Faulkner (1897–1962), 'To understand the world, you must first understand a place like Mississippi.' To learn some interesting facts about Faulkner's unique but little-known state of Mississippi, visit the site *Mississippi ... Believe It* (*http://www.mississippibelieveit.com/*). To find out more about Faulkner, visit the Faulkner site at the University of Mississippi (*http://www.mcsr.olemiss.edu/~egjbp/faulkner/faulkner.html*).

Take a real or virtual tour of a museum or cultural exhibit such as those in the *WWW Virtual Library* site, 'Museums of the World' (*http://icom.museum/vlmp/world.html*).

Origins of culture: oral tradition

Culture, the shared beliefs and practices of a people, is passed down from generation to generation. How was this information collected, stored, and retrieved before writing? It was collected and stored in the human brain and passed down by *oral tradition*. Scholars believe that memorization and recitation of human knowledge in pre-literate societies was enhanced by the use of mnemonic devices such as images, knots or beads, song or rhythm.

- Stone Age pictographs/pictures, such as those on the cave walls at Lascaux, France[6] (about 40,000 BC), were of animals and/or humans and may be related to storytelling or the passing down of hunting knowledge, tribal legends, or lore.

- The ancient Incas of Peru used a system of different knots in various colored and sized cords to record, store, and transmit information. Quipus[7] could only be interpreted by trained 'rememberers' whose knowledge has since been lost.

- The *Iliad* and the *Odyssey* are two epic stories about the last days and aftermath of the Greek/Trojan War of about 1,200 BC. The 16,000 lines of the *Iliad* and the 13,000 lines of the *Odyssey*, attributed to the blind bard Homer,[8] were passed down through oral tradition during centuries of illiteracy and not written down until about 800 BC. These tales were thought to be pure fiction until the late 1800s when German archaeologist Heinrich Schliemann uncovered the ancient city of Troy near the coast of Turkey by following Homer's literal description.[9]

  'For 3,000 years, tales of Troy and its heroes – Achilles and Hector, Paris and the legendary beauty Helen – have fired the human imagination.'[10] With *In Search of the Trojan War* (1998), Michael Wood brings vividly to life the legend and lore of the Heroic Age in an archaeological adventure that sifts through the myths and speculation to provide a privileged view of the riches and the reality of ancient Troy. Wood, who based his book on the BBC television series of the same name,[11] concludes that Mycenae and other Greek kingdoms did in fact destroy the Anatolian city of Troy at Hissarlik at the end of the Bronze Age, between 1,375 and 1,250 BC. According to the publisher's synopsis, the book is 'devoted to archeological efforts to prove the truth of Homer's epic and confirm that Troy was actually at Hissarlik. Wood also describes the history and archeology of Mycenae, where in the 1870s Heinrich Schliemann found ruins supporting Homer's description of Agamemnon's empire, Knossos and other ancient sites.'

- The author Alex Haley spent his boyhood summers in rural Tennessee listening to his grandmother and great-aunts recount tales about their family that had been handed down to them since the days of slavery. In the process of researching his family's history, which evolved into the book and mini-series *Roots: The Saga of an American Family* (1976),[12] he traveled to the village of his ancestors in Africa and heard the griote,[13] or tribal historian, recite the village history back in time. Haley recalled that his hair stood on end when the griote recounted that Kunta Kente (Haley's ancestor who was captured and sold into slavery) went hunting one day and did not return.[14]

Pictographs and ideographs

In ancient times, pictures served as mnemonic devices to help recall data and this early use of visualization led to the development of systems of symbolic pictographs and ideographs, the precursors of alphabets.

Pre-historic pictographs, literally 'picture writing,' date back to the Stone Age and, as far as is known, represent concrete objects. A related term, petroglyphs, refers to images etched in stone.[15]

Ideographs (pictures representing ideas) originated about 5,000 BC in Sumeria on clay tablets and about 4,000 BC in Egypt on papyrus.[16]

Early alphabets

Sumerian

Cuneiform, from the Latin *cuneus* or wedge, attributes its distinctive shape to the use of a wedge-shaped reed stylus to press symbols into damp clay tablets.

Cuneiform script first arose in the Tigris–Euphrates region of the Middle East (land of the Sumerians, Elamites, Akkadians, Assyrians, Hittites, Chaldeans, and Babylonians), a land known as Mesopotamia, 'land between the rivers.'

As city-states first arose in this region, a system of cylinder seals[17] to indicate ownership and pictograms to record commercial transactions developed. Over time, these symbols became more abstract and by *c.*3,000 BC had evolved into a phonetic cuneiform script.[18]

Egyptian

Thoth, who later became the ibis-headed god of scribes, is credited as the inventor of writing in Egypt. It was said that instead of being pleased, Pharaoh proclaimed this new invention would cause men's minds to grow lazy.

Egyptians called their writing *medju-netjer*, 'words of the gods,' and the Greeks later named the script, *hieroglyphica*, or 'sacred letters.' The earliest Egyptian glyphs,[19] recently discovered in the pre-dynastic tomb of Scorpion I at Abydos, have been dated to *c.*3,400–3,200 BC (yes, there really was a Scorpion King and his mace head is on exhibit at the Ashmolean Museum in Oxford, UK).[20]

Some of the oldest hieroglyphic writings in Egypt are passages from *The Book of the Dead*,[21] a compilation of burial rites, instructions, and guidance in preparation for death and the afterlife. While the oldest of these religious hieroglyphs are inscribed on tomb walls and sarcophagi, there is some evidence that as early as *c*.2,400 BC, priest scribes in Annu were producing editions on papyri.

Egyptian hieroglyphs were reserved for religious texts, and a shorthand, hieratic script was used for more common purposes. Around the seventh century BC, the writing evolved into an even simpler demotic script and the ability to translate hieroglyphs was eventually lost. In 1799, the French discovered the Rosetta Stone inscribed in three different scripts: Egyptian hieroglyphic, Egyptian demotic, and Greek. The Rosetta Stone (on display in the Egyptian Hall of the British Museum) was key to the deciphering of ancient Egyptian hieroglyphs.[22]

Greco-Roman alphabet

The knowledge of early Greek alphabets, known as Linear A and Linear B, disappeared during the Greek Dark Ages. During the Archaic Period, the Greeks adopted and adapted the Phoenician alphabet to their language.

The alphabet (named after the first two letters, *alpha* and *beta*) originated in the Middle East about 3,600 years ago, and was known as the North Semitic alphabet. The names given to the phonetic symbols were the same as those of the objects on which they were based.

The first symbol *aleph* originally represented the head of an ox. *Aleph* developed into the Greek letter *alpha*, which later became our letter *A*.

The second symbol *beth* originally represented a house. *Beth* developed into the Greek *beta*, and later our letter *B*.

The North Semitic alphabet had two offshoots:

- Aramaic, which later developed into Hebrew and Arabic;
- Caananite, which was adopted by the Phoenicians.

The Greeks adopted the Phoenician alphabet and added vowels.

The Romans modified the Greek alphabet into the one we use today. The Latin language also absorbed most of the Greek language. Today, about half of the English language has Greco-Roman roots.

The ancient Greek language is richer, more complex, and more precise than modern languages, and even the modern Koine (common) Greek is a much simplified version of Classical Greek. For many centuries, Classical Greek was the language of scholars and scientists and was a requirement, along with Latin, for higher education:

- 'I have become convinced that of all that human language has produced truly and simply beautiful, I knew nothing before I learned Greek ... Without a knowledge of Greek there is no education.' (Leo Tolstoy)

- Learn Greek; it is the language of wisdom.' (George Bernard Shaw)

- 'I would make everyone learn English; then I would let the clever ones learn Latin as an honour and Greek as a treat.' (Sir Winston Churchill)

Exercises

Exercise 1

1. Browse and read one of the entries of *The New Dictionary of Cultural Literacy* (2003) by E.D. Hirsch, Jr, Joseph F. Kett, and James Trefil, at: *http://www.bartleby.com/59/*.

2. Take one or more of the 'Cultural Literacy Tests' at the Literacy Company website: *http://www.readfaster.com/culturalliteracy/*.

Exercise 2

1. Visit a cultural exhibit near you (an art exhibit, museum exhibit, historic home). Write a brief description of the exhibit. Include the website if available.

Exercise 3

1. List 5–10 things which best illustrate the culture of your society. Why do you feel that these best illustrate your culture?

Exercise 4

1. List 3–4 current events happening in your country or town. How do these events affect the culture of your society? What is their impact on the world at large? How are these events impacted by culture?

Exercise 5

1. Five hundred visitors are coming to your community from another country. Choose 5–10 things or ideas that they would need to know about your culture in order to be 'culturally literate' in your society. These may include places, behavioral norms, vocabulary, works of art and/or literature, etc.

2. Prepare a written guide (illustrations may be included) explaining these places, ideas, norms, works of art/literature to your visitors.

Additional sources

American Historical Association: 'Why Study History?' by Peter Stearns, at:
    http://www.historians.org/pubs/Free/WhyStudyHistory.htm.
Ancestor search: *Free Dictionary of Surname Origins and Last-Name Meanings*, at:
    http://www.searchforancestors.com/surnames/origin/.
British Library: *Archival Sound Recordings*, at:
    http://sounds.bl.uk/.
The History Channel:
    http://www.history.com/.
Storytelling: Passport to Success in the 21st Century, at:
    http://www.creatingthe21stcentury.org/.

Notes

1. E.D. Hirsch (1992) *Cultural Literacy: What Every American Needs to Know.* Stuart, FL: Braille International, p. 19.
2. Geographic.org (n.d.) 'Geography Glossary,' at: *http://www.geographic.org/glossary.html* (accessed 14 January 2009).
3. National Park Service (n.d.) 'Archaeological Terms,' at: *http://www.nps.gov/history/seac/terms.htm* (accessed 25 January 2009).
4. Hirsch (1992), op. cit.
5. Robert Rosen (2000) *Global Literacies: Lessons on Leadership and National Cultures.* Darby, PA: Diane Publishing.
6. National Geographic (n.d.) 'France's Magical Cave Art,' at: *http://ngm.nationalgeographic.com/ngm/data/2001/08/01/html/ft_20010801.6.html* (accessed 25 January 2009).

7. Viviano Domenici and Davide Domenici (1996) 'Talking knots of the Inka,' *Archaeology*, 49(6), at: *http://www.archaeology.org/9611/abstracts/inka.html* (accessed 12 December 2008).
8. Richard Hooker (n.d.) 'Bureaucrats & Barbarians: The Greek Dark Ages: Homer,' at: *http://www.wsu.edu:8080/~dee/MINOA/HOMER.htm* (accessed 8 November 2007).
9. Steven Kreis (n.d.) 'Trojan War Resources,' *The History Guide, Lectures on Ancient and Medieval European History*, at: *http://www.historyguide .org/ancient/troy.html* (accessed 15 January 2009).
10. Michael Wood (1998) *In Search of the Trojan War*. Berkeley, CA: University of California Press.
11. British Broadcasting Corporation (BBC) (2004) *In Search of the Trojan War* (DVD), at: *http://www.bbcshop.com/History/In-Search-of-the-Trojan-War-DVD/invt/bbcdvd1425* (accessed 14 March 2009).
12. Alex Haley (1976) *Roots: The Saga of an American Family*. New York: Doubleday.
13. Mike Dowling (n.d.) 'A Great Oral Tradition,' at: *http://www .mrdowling.com/609ancafr.html* (accessed 7 November 2007).
14. Kunta Kinte-Alex Haley Foundation (n.d.) 'Alex Haley Biography,' at: *http://www.kintehaley.org/haleybio.html* (accessed 9 October 2008).
15. Don Austin (n.d.) 'Rock Art Gallery,' at: *http://www.petroglyphs.us/* (accessed 14 February 2009).
16. R.A. Guisepi (1999) 'Writing,' *The International History Project*, at: *http://history-world.org/writing.htm* (accessed 4 April 2009).
17. The Metropolitan Museum of Art (n.d.) 'Cylinder Seals,' *Heilbrunn Timeline of Art History*, at: *http://www.metmuseum.org/toah/hi/hi_secy.htm* (accessed 4 March 2009).
18. Lawrence Lo (n.d.) 'Ancient Scripts: Sumerian,' at: *http://www.ancientscripts .com/sumerian.html* (accessed 12 August 2008).
19. Larkin Mitchell (2008) 'Earliest Egyptian glyphs,' *Archaeology*, 52(2), at: *http://www.archaeology.org/9903/newsbriefs/egypt.html* (accessed 12 August 2008).
20. The Ashmolean Museum of Art and Archaeology (n.d.) 'The Scorpion King Mace Head,' at: *http://www.ashmolean.org/ash/faqs/q005/q005001.php* (accessed 5 May 2008).
21. E.A. Wallis Budge (1895) 'The Egyptian Book of the Dead: The Papyrus of Ani,' at: *http://www.sacred-texts.com/egy/ebod/* (accessed 5 May 2008).
22. British Museum (n.d.) 'Rosetta Stone', at: *http://www.britishmuseum.org/ explore/highlights/highlight_objects/aes/t/the_rosetta_stone.aspx* (accessed 3 June 2007).

3

Library literacy: history, types, and roles

Libraries are the memories of mankind. (Johann Wolfgang von Goethe)

Early libraries

To understand what a library is, it is useful to know the history of libraries, how they developed over time, and what traditions of the early libraries continue in modern libraries. The word *library* is from the Latin *liber*, meaning 'book,' and a library has traditionally meant a collection of books.

The related term *archive* is from the Greek *archeia*, or place of *archeion*, a public office. The origin of the root word indicates it was originally a storehouse of government records. The *Online Dictionary of Library and Information Science (ODLIS)*[1] defines *archive* as a storage facility that preserves historical, informational, legal, or evidential records. The earliest physical repositories discovered so far date to about 3,000 BC in Mesopotamia (modern Iraq) and Egypt and were associated with royal palaces and temples.

Babylonian

Cuneiform schools and libraries

The development of cuneiform script was accompanied by the founding of schools and libraries. A large cache of school tablets (dated to *c.*2,500 BC) unearthed in the ancient city of Shuruppak revealed that Sumerian schoolteachers were the first-known compilers of dictionaries (Sumero-Akkadian dictionaries signify a mingling of the two cultures).

The headmaster ('father of the school'), called *ummia* or 'teacher,' ruled over his students ('sons of the school') with the threat of corporal punishment for mistakes or laziness. Among the firsts listed by Kramer in *History Begins at Sumer: Thirty-Nine 'Firsts' in Recorded History* (1988) are the first schools, the first pharmacopoeia, and the first library catalog.[2]

Houses of tablets

Excavations in the ancient city of Nippur have uncovered libraries known as 'Houses of Tablets' with thousands of Sumerian and Akkadian inscribed tablets of administrative, legal, medical, and business records, religious and astronomical texts, and the oldest known versions (late third millennium) of literary works:

- *Epic of Gilgamesh*, the account of the quest of a hero for the secret of immortality. Gilgamesh (ruler of Uruk *c.*2,700 BC) obtains the key to immortality only to have it stolen by a serpent. The Gilgamesh story is known as 'the Sumerian Noah' due to its reference to the survivor of a great flood.[3]
- *Enuma Elish*, or 'When on high,' the Sumerian account of creation, was recited annually during the New Year Celebration, probably from atop the ziggurat (temple).[4]

Hammurabi, ruler of Babylon (1,792–1,750 BC) amassed a large collection of clay tablets containing hymns, divination texts (reading the future from the entrails of animals), mathematical texts, and myths. Hammurabi is most notable for writing the oldest inscribed law code found thus far, *The Code of Hammurabi*:

- to cause justice to prevail in the country;
- to destroy the wicked and the evil;
- that the strong may not oppress the weak.

The *Code of Hammurabi* is engraved on a basalt stele and is on display at the Louvre in Paris.[5]

First librarian

Ashurbanipal, king of Assyria in the seventh century BC, is considered by historians to be the first great librarian. His House of Tablets was divided into two sections: one, an archive of government documents, business records, and correspondence; the other, a collection of literature and scholarly works of history, religion, science, mathematics, astrology, and medicine. The collection of more than 25,000 tablets was arranged by subject.

Ashurbanipal sent agents to search the empire for scholarly works and literature to be copied and annotated by his royal scribes. This is believed to be the first attempt to create a great universal library and was said to be the inspiration for Alexander's Great Library.

Of his great library at Ninevah, Ashurbanipal stated:

> I obtained the hidden treasures of the sum of the scribes' knowledge ... I have read the artistic script of the Sumerians and the obscure script of the Akkadians and I have deciphered the inscriptions that were carved in the rock some time before the Flood.[6]

Egyptian

Egyptian houses of writings

Egypt is credited with the invention of books in the form of *papyrus*, a lightweight writing material later adopted by the Greeks and Romans. Papyrus reeds that grew plentifully along the Nile were processed into sheets and rolled into scrolls. The earliest fragment of papyrus (from which our word *paper* is derived) dates to c.3,000 BC and the oldest papyrus with hieroglyphic text to c.2,400 BC.

One of the earliest historical references to an Egyptian library, c.2,470 BC, was a tomb inscription that referred to the owner as a 'Scribe in the House of Books.' In the fourth and fifth dynasties (c.2,600–2,300 BC), Egypt had at least three royal 'Houses of Writings,' which held archives, tax records, and religious texts, and there is some evidence to support Egyptian libraries as far back as 3,000 BC.

King Ramses II (1,300 BC) had a large library of over 20,000 papyrus scrolls containing works of history, science, and literature. Popular literature of the time included such tales as 'Story of the Eloquent Peasant,' 'Tale of the Shipwrecked Sailor,' and 'Tale of Two Brothers.'[7]

Egyptian literature

One of the most popular stories, dating back to c.2,000 BC was 'The Story of Sinuhe' (called the Egyptian Moses). (An interesting note is that

'The Story of Sinuhe' was adapted by Hollywood for the epic *The Egyptian* (1954).[8])

Greek

Classical periods

Much of the traditions and culture of Western civilization may be traced back to the Greeks – many scholars believe that even the Renaissance was influenced by the rediscovery of Greek logic and literature.

The Classical Greek period was an era of widespread literacy and intense interest in art and architecture, science, mathematics, music, history, athletics, philosophy, theater, and literature.

There is evidence of public libraries in Greece around the sixth century BC, in addition to the private collections of scholars and playwrights.

- Pisistratus, ruler of Athens, founded what Aulus Gellius calls 'the first public library' in 560 BC.[9]

- About the same time, Polycrates, tyrant of Samos, founded a public library on the island.[10]

Bookshops and scriptoria (where clerks copied works of literature on commission) were common in Classical Athens, particularly in the agora, or public marketplace.

- In *The Birds* (414 BC), Aristophanes portrayed Athenians as voracious readers who rushed out to the bookshops each morning to browse and chat with their friends.

- In *The Frogs*, one of Aristophanes' characters comments, 'You must be very unobservant, or very uneducated; you don't even know your Aesop.'

Private literary collections became status symbols of the literati: Nicocrates of Cyprus, Euclid the Archon, Euripides, Euthydemus, and Aristotle.

Greek education reflected their ideals of 'a sound mind in a sound body' (a balance of mental and physical fitness) and 'know thyself' (logic and self-reflection). While girls were educated at home, usually by slaves, boys were educated more formally in *gymnasia*, where they were trained in athletics and taught Homer and Aesop as well as the seven liberal arts:

- *Trivium*: grammar, rhetoric, logic;

- *Quadrivium*: geometry, arithmetic, music, astronomy.

These subjects were called the liberal arts from the root word of liberty, *liber*, reflecting the Greeks' view that a free, democratic society (which to them meant freeborn male citizens) depended on a literate populace.

Hellenistic period

When Alexander the Great died in 323 BC, he left a vast empire that was apportioned to his three generals. The general Ptolemy took control of Egypt, founding the last Egyptian dynasty.

In 295 BC, Pharoah Ptolemy I Sotor established the Great Library of Alexandria, Egypt. At the adjoining Museion, scholars made notable advances in the fields of mathematics, astronomy, geometry, applied science, and medicine, taking advantage of the observatory, zoo, and botanical gardens in the grounds.

- Zenodotus was the first librarian at the Great Library of Alexandria and the first known to put lists in alphabetical order.
- Ptolemy II Philadelphus collected scrolls from all parts of Greece and Asia. Resident scholars wrote, translated foreign works, and gathered compilations of other manuscripts. Officials traveled through the region, purchasing entire collections for the library.
- Callimachus compiled the first bibliography of Greek literature, *Pinakes*, or *Tables* (120 volumes).[11]

Ptolemy III Euergetes asked world leaders to lend him their scrolls and even ordered a search of all ships for scrolls. These scrolls would be confiscated and replaced by copies.

Every known scholarly work of the ancient world was collected and translated into Greek. Considered to be the greatest library of the ancient world (500,000–700,000 scrolls), it was destroyed by a series of fires, the first of which occurred in 47 BC during Caesar's invasion of Cleopatra's Egypt.[12]

The Great Library at Alexandria was the second known attempt to establish a universal library (Ashurbanipal's Great Library at Ninevah being the first). The scholar Leibnitz revived this idea during the Renaissance.

In modern times, the largest and most comprehensive libraries are the US Library of Congress (*http://www.loc.gov/*) and the British Library (*http://www.bl.uk/*), with many millions of items – books, manuscripts (handwritten books), incunabula (early printed books), photographs, recordings, and maps.

Today, the Egyptian government is trying to restore the former glory of the great library, the Bibliotheca Alexandrina.[13]

Selected Greek glossary

Arete: Virtue, excellence, goodness.

Bibliotheke: Bookcase; later came to mean a library.

Gymnasium: Literally 'to exercise naked,' a school for boys to physically exercise, as well as be taught the seven liberal arts.

Lyceum: Covered walk next to the Temple of Apollo the Wolf Slayer where Aristotle taught philosophy. Later came to mean a school.

Museion: Temple of the Muses; museum.

Classical Rome

According to the Roman poet Horace, 'Greece has conquered her rude conqueror,' meaning that, although the Romans conquered Greece, they admired and absorbed Greek language, literature, art, and culture.

- The first Roman libraries were private collections plundered from the Greeks as spoils of war.

- There is a record of Roman bookshops, *taberna libraria*, in the Forum, or public marketplace.

- As with the Greeks, private libraries were usually specialized collections.[14]

- Excavations at the Villa of Papyri at Herculaneum (a seaside resort near Pompeii) revealed a private library of about 1,800 scrolls, primarily the works of the philosopher Philodemus.[15]

Rome carried on the Greek tradition of public libraries:

- The first public library in Rome was planned by Julius Caesar and built by Asinius Pollio *c.*39 BC on the Palatine Hill.

- Julius Caesar's concept of adjoining 'sister' Latin and Greek libraries, *Bybliotheka Latina Apollinis* and *Bybliotheca Graeca Apollinis*, was planned by the Roman scholar Varro who had written *De Bibliothecis (On Libraries)*.[16]

The first Roman Emperor, Augustus, established a public library in the Temple of Apollo on the Palatine Hill, and another, the *Bibliotheca Octaviana*, in the Porticus Octavia.

The Emperor Vespasian founded the *Bibliotheca Pacis* (Library of Peace) in the Temple of Peace; the library was dedicated in AD 75 and considered by Pliny to be one of the three most beautiful buildings in Rome. The greatest imperial library was built in the Forum of Trajan by the Emperor Trajan. The two libraries of the *Bibliotheca Ulpia*, founded in AD 114, faced one another across a courtyard, the Latin collection on the west and the Greek on the east.[17]

The Romans made some unique contributions to librarianship:

- Trajan was the earliest known Roman emperor to build a bath-house library. Other notable public baths or *thermae* include the Baths of Caracalla and the Baths of Diocletian, which could hold up to 6,000 bathers.[18]

- Roman libraries were spacious rooms lined with wall niches that held numbered wooden bookcases, *armaria*, leaving space in the center of the room for reading tables and chairs. Those in charge of the libraries were called *librarii a bibliotheca*, or librarians.[19]

- By *c.* AD 150, the Romans were replacing papyrus scrolls with codices, early books of parchment or vellum sheets (made from animal skins) laced together accordian-style, with wood or leather covers. The codex had several advantages over scrolls: they were more portable and easier to reference, store, and read.

To understand the influence of Rome on Western culture, even before the Christian era, one must be aware of the history of Roman Britain. Britannia was a Roman province for almost 400 years and its major town was Londinium (present-day London). More about historic Roman London can be found at the Museum of London (*http://www.museumoflondon.org.uk/English/Collections/Prehistoric1700/Roman.htm*).

Bath in England was once the Roman town known as Aquae Sulis ('Waters of Sul' or 'Minerva'), named after a sacred, hot spring (*http://www.romanbaths.co.uk/*).

Latin literature and language

- One of the most important works of Latin literature was *The Aeneid* (19 BC), the tale of Aeneas, who escaped death when Troy fell to the Greeks. According to the epic, Aeneas, along with his son and elderly father, emigrated to Italy and founded the Roman race whose destiny was to rule the world in peace and prosperity (*Pax Romana*).

- Virgil was commissioned to write *The Aeneid* by the Emperor Augustus to glorify Rome through a Homeric-style epic that celebrated the mythical founding and destiny of the Roman Empire.

- The poet Horace's most famous works, *Odes* (23 BC), praised the simple life of the Roman countryside.

- Livy, a Roman historian, wrote the 142 volume *Ab Urbe Condita* (*From the Founding of the City*) (begun in 29 BC).

- Suetonius, a biographer, historian, and author of *Lives of the Twelve Caesars* (*c.* AD 121), served as imperial librarian under Hadrian. The BBC mini-series, *I, Claudius* was largely based on the works of Suetonius.[20]

Latin mottos

Novum ordo seclorum, 'A new order of the ages (is created)' – motto on the Great Seal of the US.
Annuit coeptis, '(He) has favored our undertaking' – motto on reverse of Great Seal of US and on the $1 bill.
E pluribus unum, 'Out of many (states), one (nation)' – motto of the USA.
Virtute et armis, 'By valor and arms' – Mississippi state motto.

Selected Latin words and phrases

alma mater: one's undergraduate university (lit. nourishing mother)
alter ego: another self
ante bellum: before the war
bona fide: in good faith
c. (*circa*): about
cf. (*confer*): compare
e.g. (*exempli gratia*): for (the sake of) example
et al. (*et alia*): and others
etc. (*et cetera*): and so forth
ex libris: from the books or library of
ibid. (*ibidem*): in the same place
i.e. (*id est*): that is
magna cum laude: with great praise or honor
NB (*nota bene*): note well
op. cit. (*opere citato*): in the work cited

per se: essentially (lit. by itself)

quid pro quo: something in exchange (lit. something for something)

q.v. (*quod vide*): which see (used for cross-references)

scientia est potentia: knowledge is power

sine qua non: an indispensable condition (lit. without which not)

summa cum laude: with highest praise or honor

tabula rasa: a clean slate

tempus fugit: time flies

terra firma: dry land

terra incognita: unknown land

vice versa: conversely (lit. the change being turned)

vita brevis, ars longa: life is short, art is long

vox populi: voice of the people

Medieval scriptorium

Medieval is Latin for Middle Ages, so called because it is the period between the ancient and modern worlds. It is generally dated from the fall of Rome in 476 AD until the Renaissance.

In the Islamic East, literature and libraries flourished, but in the West, the Medieval or Middle Ages are also known as the Dark Ages because of widespread illiteracy. During this time Holy Scriptures, as well as classical literature and scholarly works, were preserved and copied in monastic scriptoria. *Scriptoria* is the plural form of *scriptorium*, which is a room in a monastery set aside for the copying, writing, or illumination of manuscripts and records.

Name of the Rose by Umberto Eco is a murder mystery set in a medieval monastery and scriptorium where monks laboriously copied texts by hand on parchment or vellum. *Name of the Rose*, a 1986 movie based on the book, starred Sean Connery, Christian Slater, and F. Murray Abraham.[21]

Since most medieval Europeans were illiterate, alternative methods were used to teach the Bible: Gothic cathedrals, such as Canterbury Cathedral (*http://www.canterbury-cathedral.org/*), were constructed with biblical stories illustrated in sculpture and stained glass and biblical Miracle or Mystery Plays were enacted.[22]

Beowulf (*http://www.humanities.mcmaster.ca/~beowulf/*) is an epic tale dated to 1000 AD. A modern retelling of Beowulf was published by Michael Crichton as *Eaters of the Dead* (1976). A movie based on the book and starring Antonio Banderas was called *The 13th Warrior*.[23] A computer-enhanced version of *Beowulf* was released in 2007.[24]

Types of libraries

School libraries

School libraries contain materials that support the school's curriculum.

One interesting example of a large free public school for children during the Victorian era was the Ragged School in London (*http://www.raggedschoolmuseum.org.uk/nextgen/history/schoolhistory.shtml*).

Public libraries

Public libraries contain materials that support general research, recreational reading, community information needs, and local history. The first public library since ancient times (with a small subscription fee) was the Library Company of Philadelphia, established by Benjamin Franklin in 1731.[25]

One great champion of public libraries was Andrew Carnegie, who funded the building of more than 2,500 public libraries in the English-speaking world. The first Carnegie Library is in his birthplace, Dunfermline, Scotland,[26] and the first Carnegie Library in the States is in his adopted hometown of Pittsburgh, Pennsylvania (*http://www.clpgh.org/*).

Academic libraries

Academic libraries contain materials that support both general research and the specific programs and degrees offered at the institution. The first great university and academic library in the Western world is the University of Bologna, Italy.[27] The University of Oxford, the first great English university with the oldest English-language library, the Bodleian, was based on the Bologna University model.[28] The first university library in the US was the Harvard University Library, founded in 1638.[29]

Archives and special collections

Archives and special collections contain materials that are being collected for long-term preservation. Examples include the US National Archives and Records Administration (NARA: *http://www.archives.gov/*), the British National Archives (*http://www.nationalarchives.gov.uk/*), and the Folger Shakespeare Library (*http://www.folger.edu/*) in Washington, DC.

Special libraries

Special libraries contain materials that are very specific to the needs of the institution. These are generally not open to the public and include libraries in corporations and institutions such as prisons and hospitals (see the Special Libraries Association at *http://www.sla.org/*).

National libraries

The British Museum Library was established in 1753 when Sir Hans Sloan bequeathed his large collection of books and manuscripts to the nation. In 1973, the British Library (*http://www.bl.uk/*) was founded as a separate institution and is now housed in a modern building near King's Cross/St Pancras Station.

The Bibliothèque Nationale of France (*http://www.bnf.fr/*), originally the Royal Library founded by Charles V in the fourteenth century, was established in 1789 after the French Revolution as the National Library of the French people.

The US National Library, the Library of Congress (*http://www.loc.gov/*), was established in 1800 as a reference library for Congress. Thomas Jefferson sold his large and valuable book collection to the Library of Congress in 1814, more than doubling the collection.[30]

Roles of libraries

What is the role of the library in a democratic society?

- To collect and preserve information.
- To provide access to information.

Why is that important?

- If information is not preserved, it is lost.
- The old adage is true – knowledge is power and information is the means to succeed. Democracy is based on freedom and equality, and when access to information is limited or denied according to one individual's or group's beliefs, the rest of society, including future generations, may suffer.

Libraries provide access to information:

- by organizing information – by creating, improving on, and implementing classification schemes and cataloging tools, librarians organize information so that specific items can be located;
- by selecting, purchasing, and maintaining materials so that they are accessible to others.

Exercises

Exercise 1

1. Find an article or website about an ancient library or collection.
2. Write a summary of the information including the name of the library or collection as well as the language, format, and content of the items in the collection.

Exercise 2

1. What is the name of a Carnegie library in your state or area?
2. Write a brief description of the library including when it was founded.

Exercise 3

1. What is the name and location of the nearest public library?
2. What is the online address (URL)?
3. What are some examples of services or programs offered at the library?

Exercise 4

1. What is the name and location of your national library?
2. What is the online address (URL)?
3. What are some examples of items in their collection?

Exercise 5

1. What is the name and physical location of a national library other than your own?
2. What is the online address (URL)?
3. What are some examples of items in their collection?

Additional sources

Timeline of the History of Information:
   http://people.ischool.berkeley.edu/~nunberg/timeline.html
Cuneiform Digital Library Initiative:
   http://cdli.ucla.edu/
'Were Egyptians the First Scribes?' BBC news article:
   http://news.bbc.co.uk/1/hi/sci/tech/235724.stm
The History of Ancient Egyptian Writing, by Marie Parsons:
   http://www.touregypt.net/featurestories/writing.htm
The Greeks: Crucible of Civilization:
   http://www.pbs.org/empires/thegreeks/htmlver/
Classical Language Instruction Project:
   http://www.princeton.edu/~clip/
Chaucer's *Canterbury Tales*:
   http://www.uwm.edu/Library/special/exhibits/clastext/clspg073.htm
Digital Scriptorium:
   http://www.scriptorium.columbia.edu/
The Virtual Abbey: A Medieval Tour
   http://www.newyorkcarver.com/Abbey.htm
Labyrinth: Resources:
   http://www8.georgetown.edu/departments/medieval/labyrinth/labyrinth-home.html
Types of Libraries, American Library Association:
   http://www.ala.org/ala/educationcareers/careers/librarycareerssite/typesoflibraries.cfm

Notes

1. Joan M. Reitz (n.d.) *ODLIS – Online Dictionary of Library and Information Science*, at: *http://lu.com/odlis/* (accessed 8 July 2007).
2. Samuel Noah Kramer (1988) *History Begins at Sumer: Thirty-Nine Firsts in Recorded History*. Philadelphia: University of Pennsylvania Press.

3. Richard Hooker (1996) *Epic of Gilgamesh*, at: *http://www.wsu.edu/~dee/MESO/GILG.HTM* (accessed 20 April 2008).

4. John Paul Adams (2008) *The Enuma Elish*, at: *http://www.csun.edu/~hcfll004/enuma.html* (accessed 23 January 2008).

5. Louvre Museum (n.d.) 'A Closer Look at the Code of Hammurabi,' at: *http://www.louvre.fr/llv/dossiers/detail_oal.jsp?CONTENT%3C%3Ecnt_id=10134198673229909&CURRENT_LLV_OAL%3C%3Ecnt_id=10134 198673229909&bmLocale=en* (accessed 5 July 2009).

6. Leroy Waterman (1931) *Royal Correspondence of the Assyrian Empire*. Ann Arbor, MI: University of Michigan Press.

7. Lionel Casson (2002) *Libraries in the Ancient World*. New Haven, CT: Yale University Press.

8. Internet Movie Database (IMDB), *The Egyptian*, at: *http://www.imdb.com/title/tt0046949/* (accessed 8 September 2008).

9. Public Broadcasting Service (PBS) (n.d.) 'Psistratus Rules as Tyrant and Reforms the Economy,' *The Greeks: Crucible of Civilization*, at: *http://www.pbs.org/empires/thegreeks/background/6_p1.html* (accessed 24 May 2007).

10. Tim Spalding (n.d.) 'Polycrates,' *Dictionary of Greek and Roman Biography and Mythology*, at: *http://www.ancientlibrary.com/smith-bio/2793.html* (accessed 5 June 2008).

11. Casson (2002), op. cit.

12. Matthew Battles (2004) *Library: An Unquiet History*. W.W. Norton.

13. Bibliotheca Alexandrina – see: *http://www.bibalex.org/English/index.aspx* (accessed 1 August 2008).

14. Casson (2002), op. cit.

15. University of California Los Angeles (UCLA) (n.d.) 'The Philodemus Project,' at: *http://www.humnet.ucla.edu/humnet/classics/philodemus/philhome.htm* (accessed 7 June 2007).

16. Casson (2002), op. cit.

17. Ibid.

18. Public Broadcasting Service (PBS) (n.d.) 'The Baths of Caracalla,' *NOVA: Lost Empires*, at: *http://www.pbs.org/wgbh/nova/lostempires/roman/day.html* (accessed 8 November 2007).

19. Michael H. Harris (1999) *History of Libraries of the Western World*. Lanham, MD: Scarecrow Press.

20. Saint Anselm College (n.d.) *I Claudius Project*, at: *http://www.anselm.edu/internet/classics/I,CLAUDIUS/* (accessed 1 July 2007).

21. Internet Movie Database (IMDB) (n.d.) 'Der Name der Rose,' at: *http://www.imdb.com/title/tt0091605/* (accessed 5 July 2008).

22. University of Victoria (n.d.) 'The Mystery Plays,' at: *http://internetshakespeare.uvic.ca/Library/SLT/stage/mysteries.html* (accessed 3 June 2008).

23. Internet Movie Database (IMDB) (n.d.) *The 13th Warrior*, at: *http://www.imdb.com/title/tt0120657/* (accessed 7 July 2008).

24. Internet Movie Database (IMDB) (n.d.) *Beowulf*, at: *http://www.imdb.com/title/tt0442933/* (7 July 2008).

25. Library Company of Philadelphia (n.d.) 'About LCP,' at: *http://www.librarycompany.org/about/* (accessed 28 July 2009).

26. Fife Council (n.d.) 'Dunfermline Library,' at: *http://www.fifedirect.org.uk/topics/index.cfm?fuseaction=facility.display&subjectid=F6E580D1-E419-48D7-BCF2BB754F5E949F&FacId=0C95F6FA-11D6-467F-BDE5ED42118689F4&print=true* (accessed 6 July 2009).
27. University of Bologna (n.d.) 'Our History,' at: *http://www.eng.unibo.it/PortaleEn/University/Our+History/* (accessed 28 July 2009).
28. University of Oxford (n.d.) 'History of the Bodleian Library,' at: *http://www.ouls.ox.ac.uk/bodley/about/history* (accessed 28 July 2009).
29. Harvard University (n.d.) 'Early History of Harvard University,' *The Harvard Guide: History, Lore, and More*, at: *http://www.news.harvard.edu/guide/intro/index.html* (accessed 28 July 2009).
30. James H. Billington (n.d.) 'Jefferson's legacy: a brief history of the Library of Congress,' at: *http://www.loc.gov/loc/legacy/preface.html* (accessed 28 July 2008).

4

Library literacy: information sources, classification systems

Classification, broadly defined, is the act of organizing the universe of knowledge into some systematic order. It has been considered the most fundamental activity of the human mind. (Lois Mai Chan)[1]

In addition to classical and popular literature (fiction), libraries contain non-fiction. Non-fiction by definition presents factual narratives about the world but how *valid* and *reliable* is the information presented? ... That depends on the *source*.

Research indicates that the greatest weakness related to information literacy is the inability of most people to judge information quality. By understanding the types of information sources and how they are related in the information cycle, one can become a more educated consumer of information.

Information source types

There are three basic types of non-fiction information: *primary*, *secondary*, and *tertiary*:

- *Primary source* information is original, first-hand information, direct and reliable:
  - eyewitness accounts produced at or near the time of the event such as diaries, letters, images, and first-hand reports in newspapers;
  - original documents such as the Magna Carta or Declaration of Independence;
  - original research such as scholarly, peer-reviewed journal articles;
  - government reports such as census reports.

- *Secondary* information, or second-hand information, is information that is filtered or interpreted:
  - textbooks, general encyclopedias and other reference sources, popular magazines;
  - any information that is not primary, original information.
- *Tertiary*, or third-hand information, contains little or no information but points or leads to sources of information:
  - indexes, abstracts (brief summaries of books or articles);
  - bibliographies (citation list);
  - other finding aids.

What primary sources can be found in libraries?

Primary source information, the most reliable type of information that can be found in a library, includes:

- scholarly books;
- scholarly journal articles;
- government reports;
- archival materials such as historic images, maps, manuscripts, diaries, journals, and newspapers.

What secondary and tertiary sources can be found in libraries?

Secondary and tertiary source information, useful for background information and as finding aids to further information, includes books that interpret information such as textbooks and other non-fiction books that are not primary sources, reference books, and reference sources.

What is a reference source?

A reference book presents information in a condensed manner. Reference sources may have entries arranged in alphabetical order that are signed by the author or unsigned. Entries that are authored and signed by an authority are more reliable than those that are unsigned.

Reference books are usually either secondary or tertiary sources and many sources are available in print and online. The value of using reference resources in a library is that they are evaluated by librarians and subject specialists who choose quality, reliable reference resources for their patrons.

Types of reference sources

Almanac

An almanac is an annual compendium of useful data and statistics relating to countries, personalities, events, subjects, etc. For example:

- general almanacs: *World Almanac and Book of Facts*
- subject-specific almanacs: *Almanac of American Politics*
- online: *Information Please* (*http://www.infoplease.com*)

Directory

A directory is a list of people or organizations, systematically arranged, usually in alphabetical order, giving addresses, affiliations, etc. for individuals, and addresses, officers, functions, and similar data for organizations. For example:

- general directory: telephone directory
- online: switchboard.com (*http://www.switchboard.com*)
- subject-specific: *American Library Directory*

Annual/yearbook

An annual/yearbook is an annual compendium of images, facts, statistics, etc., about events of the preceding year, often limited to a specific country, institution, discipline, or subject. For example:

- general yearbook: *Grolier Encyclopedia Yearbook*
- subject-specific yearbook: *UK Civil Service Yearbook*, available online (*http://www.opsi.gov.uk/official-publications/civil-service-year-book.htm*)

Handbook/manual

A handbook/manual is a small, portable, hand-sized book that provides concise factual information on a specific subject, organized for quick and easy access. For example:

- subject-specific: *Statistical Handbook on the American Family*
- print and online: *Occupational Outlook Handbook*, which lists career information by occupation (*http://www.bls.gov/oco/*)

Biographical dictionary

A biographical dictionary is a single- or multi-volume offering containing biographical summaries. For example:

- general bio-dictionary: *Webster's Biographical Dictionary*
- subject-specific: *Biographical Dictionary of the History of Technology, American National Biography, Contemporary Black Biography, Biographical Dictionary of Ancient Greek and Roman Women*

Marquis Who's Who is a major publisher of biographical directories and has a list of print and online publications (*http://www.marquiswhoswho .com/products/print_directories.asp*).

Dictionary/glossary

Dictionaries deal with all aspects of words including definitions, spelling, syllabication, punctuation, usage, and etymology (origin). For example:

- the most famous general dictionary: *Oxford English Dictionary (OED)* (recommended reading is Simon Winchester (1999) *The Professor and the Madman: A Tale of Murder, Insanity, and the Making of the OED*,[2] a true story of one of the major contributors to the *OED* (an American doctor who was criminally insane) which reads like a murder mystery and offers fascinating insight into the tremendous scholarly effort of compiling and publishing the *OED*)
- subject-specific print dictionary: *Dictionary of American Slang*
- online: *http://www.dictionary.com*

Encyclopedia

An encyclopedia is a book or set of books containing summary, short essays on a variety of topics usually arranged alphabetically. An entry may be signed or unsigned with or without illustration or a list of references for further reading. For example:

- general: *Encyclopedia Americana*

- subject-specialist: *Encyclopedia of Bad Taste*, *Encyclopedia of Social Work*

- print and online: *Encyclopedia Britannica* (*http://www.britannica .com/*)

Atlas/gazetteer

An atlas/gazetteer is a collection of maps of places and related information

- general atlas: *National Atlas of the U.S.* (*http://www.britannica .com/*)

- historical atlas: *Atlas of Ancient Greece* (*http://www.wsu.edu: 8080/~dee/GREATLAS.HTM*)

- geographical dictionary: *U.S. Gazetteer* (*http://www.census.gov/cgi-bin/gazetteer*)

Guidebook

Travel guides are usually limited to a region or country and emphasize routes, accommodation, restaurants, and places of interest. For example:

- online: *Lonely Planet* (*http://www.lonelyplanet.com*)

Bibliography

While one usually thinks of a bibliography as a list of 'References' or 'Works Cited' in a research paper, it has an alternative meaning: a guide or list of materials to assist a user in identifying, locating, or selecting material (tertiary source). A bibliography may be a list of citations to relevant materials or it may be annotated with a brief description of content accompanying each citation.

Subject bibliography

For example:

- *Information Sources in Politics and Political Science: A Survey Worldwide*
- *True Crime Narratives: An Annotated Bibliography*

Index/abstracts

- An index is an alphabetical listing of materials.
- An abstract is a brief summary of content.

Many print indexes and abstracts have been replaced by online databases. (See Chapter 6 on network literacy for more information about databases.)

Concordance

An alphabetically arranged index of the principal words or selected words in a text, or in the works of an author, giving the precise location of each word in the text, with a brief indication of its context.

- A glossarial concordance includes a brief definition of each term.
- Concordances are usually devoted to very well-known works, such as the Bible (*http://www.blueletterbible.org*), or the works of Shakespeare (*http://www.opensourceshakespeare.org/concordance/*).

Discography

A list or catalog of audio-recordings, usually of works by a specific artist, of a certain style or genre, or of a specific time period. Each entry includes some descriptive elements: title, composer, performer(s), date of recording, release date. For example:

- Beatles discography: *http://www.aboutthebeatles.com/discography.php*.

Filmography

A list of motion pictures, usually limited to works by a specific director or performer, in a particular genre, of a specific time period or country, or on a given subject, usually listed alphabetically by title or chronologically by release date. Entries in a filmography may include some of the following descriptive elements: producer, director, cast, release date, running time, language, color or black-and-white format. For example:

- Hitchcock and other filmography categories are available at the Internet Movie Database (*http://www.imdb.com*).

How are resources organized and arranged in a library or archive?

Library materials are primarily organized by *format* (such as books, periodicals audio, video, microforms), or type (government documents, reference works, maps/atlases), then by size or subject. In some larger libraries where books are stored in areas not accessible to patrons, such as research or reference libraries, books may be arranged by size for efficient use of space and retrieved for the patron by librarians.

In most libraries where the stacks (book shelves) are accessible to patrons, books are arranged by subject with only the very large books shelved in a separate section. Materials may also be divided by *genre* (children's books, young adult books, fiction, non-fiction, etc.) or alphabetical order by author's last name.

Archival materials or special collections are typically in a separate space, ranging from a single drawer or cabinet of historical or specialized materials in a small library to a large archive or special collections department within a larger library to a large archival repository as a separate institution. Many archival collections have their own unique classification system and have finding aids to help patrons find materials.

How are resources classified and cataloged in a library or archive?

Each item in a library or archive has a unique identification number or call number and is listed in a library catalog or in archival finding aids. If the library has open stacks (bookshelves that patrons can browse), then the call number is like an address that can help patrons locate the item. A library catalog is a list of a library's holdings that includes the call number and other descriptive information for each item.

Before the electronic era, libraries had three categories of index cards (each book was indexed by title, subject, and author). Most libraries today list their holdings in an online public access catalog (OPAC) and most of these OPACs have names such as ANNA, the OPAC at Southern Mississippi Cook Library, which is named after their first librarian, Anna Roberts.

OPACs can generally be searched by author, title, subject, or keyword, and the results retrieved will be a list of items including call number, location, and whether the item is available.

Classification is the systematic arrangement of books or other materials, usually by subject matter. The purpose of classification is to provide a basis for organizing books and materials so that they may be found quickly and easily by patrons and it is also a means of grouping materials on the same subject together for the convenience of the patron.

Main classification systems

The two classification systems used by libraries are the Dewey Decimal System (DDS) and the Library of Congress (LC) Classification System. The DDS, invented in 1873 by Melvin Dewey, is a numeric system (000–999) used primarily in school and public libraries. A modified form of DDS is also used in some large academic and reference libraries such as the University of Oxford Bodleian Library and the British Library.

Dewey Decimal System

000   Generalities
100   Philosophy and psychology
200   Religion
300   Social sciences
400   Language
500   Natural sciences and mathematics
600   Technology (applied sciences)
700   The arts (fine and decorative)
800   Literature and rhetoric
900   Geography and history

Library of Congress Classification System

The LC Classification System (*http://www.loc.gov/catdir/cpso/lcco/*), originally designed in 1897 for congressional use, is now widely used by academic and research libraries worldwide. LC main class numbers consist of 21 letters of the alphabet (no I or O because they resemble the numerals 1 and 0; W, X, and Y are reserved for future subjects):

A   – General Works
B   – Philosophy, Psychology, Religion
C   – Auxiliary Sciences of History
D   – World History and History of Europe, Asia, Africa, Australia, New Zealand, etc.
E, F – History of the Americas
G   – Geography, Anthropology, Recreation
H   – Social Sciences
J   – Political Science
K   – Law
L   – Education
M   – Music and Books on Music
N   – Fine Arts
P   – Language and Literature
Q   – Science
R   – Medicine
S   – Agriculture
T   – Technology
U   – Military Science
V   – Naval Science
Z   – Bibliography, Library Science, Information Resources

Principle subdivisions are denoted by adding a letter (PR = English Literature; PS = American Literature).

- Class numbers may be subdivided precisely into very specific topics.
- Each main class was subdivided by experts in that subject, so each main class is subdivided differently.
  - Further subdivisions use Arabic numerals (PN44.M3 = Masterplots, M3 = author #).
  - Numbers after the decimal are read decimally (PN1993.56 comes before PN1993.6).

Superintendent of Documents Classification System

The US government classification system is known as the Superintendent of Documents (SuDoc) system and consists of agency letter, sub-agency number, series letter/number, report number. For instance:

- 'A' is for Agriculture Department, so Agriculture Yearbook is 'A 1.10.'

- 'X' and 'Y' are reserved for Congress and 'Z' is not used (*http:// www.access.gpo.gov/su_docs/fdlp/pubs/explain.html*).

United Nations Classification System

The United Nations classification system is by geographical region: Africa, North America, South America, Asia, Europe, and Oceania. For more information, see the UN website: *http://unstats.un.org/unsd/cr/ ctryreg/*.

How can one search for materials in a library or archive?

A library catalog is a listing of all the items within a library. In pre-computer times, library books were indexed in card catalogs which were cabinets of drawers of index cards: author cards, title cards, and subject cards. Today, this information is available in digital format – the online public access catalog (OPAC) – that allows for searching not only by author, title, or subject, but by identification number or keyword, which searches all the indexing fields. OPACs typically include items other than books, such as DVDs, microfilm, audio or talking books, and periodical titles (magazines, journals).

Examples of freely accessible online library catalogs include the Library of Congress Online Catalog (*http://catalog.loc.gov/*) and the British Library OPAC (*http://www.bl.uk/*). Each item in an online catalog contains the identification or call number of the item, where the item is located, and whether the item is available. Some public libraries offer an online service that allows patrons to reserve or hold items for the patron to pick up.

Archives and special collections are indexed and accessed in a different manner and have finding aids to help researchers. Many archives and special collections contain many collections. Finding aids or guides usually include a description of the person or organization that produced the collection and an inventory of the boxes in the collection.

Archives, special collections, and reference libraries do not allow their collections to circulate or leave the building. The items must be used on-site in supervised reading rooms. Copies of the materials can usually be made for a copy fee. To increase access and reduce handling of rare or historic materials, many libraries and archives are digitizing materials.

Exercises

Exercise 1

1. Look at the titles or descriptions of the following sources and classify them as either primary, secondary, or tertiary.

   - *Encyclopedia of Adult Education*
   - *Chemical Abstracts*
   - Painting of Monet's *Water Lilies*
   - A map of North America with the Native American tribes listed, produced the by US Department of the Interior
   - *Webster's Collegiate Dictionary*
   - *Anne Frank: The Diary of a Young Girl*

Exercise 2

Go to *Information Please* and answer the following:

1. Click on the person who is listed under 'Today's Birthdays' (see below). Who else has a birthday on this day? Fill in the month and date for 'Who shares *your* birthday?' and name at least two people who share your birthday.

Figure 4.1   *Information Please* website

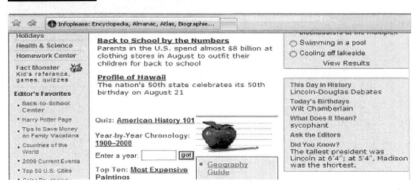

2. Also in *Information Please*, click on 'World & News' and choose a country other than your own. List the following:

   - the country, its population;
   - the ruler, the three largest cities;
   - the major language(s) spoken there.

3. Look under 'Health and Science' then 'Disease and Mortality' and click on 'Life Expectancy for Countries.'

   - Which country has the highest life expectancy? What is the life expectancy?
   - Which country has the lowest life expectancy? What is the life expectancy?

4. Click on 'Leading Causes of Mortality Throughout the World, 2002.' What were the top three leading causes of mortality?

5. Using the S9.com biographical dictionary (*http://www.s9.com/*), answer the following questions:

   - When was Mary Tudor born? How long did she live?
   - In what sport did Jayne Torvill and Christopher Dean win an Olympic gold medal? In what year did they win the medal? Where were the Olympics held that year?
   - Who was Theodor Geisel?

6. Using one of the online dictionaries, answer the following questions:

   - Are you perspicacious?
   - If your cat is doing his/her ablutions, what is he/she doing?
   - List three synonyms for the word irrepressible.

   Go to the *Online Slang Dictionary* (*http://onlineslangdictionary .com/*) and choose 'Browse by Letter.' Choose a letter and then choose three words that are unknown to you. What do they mean? If you gaffle a car, what have you done?

7. Go to Wikipedia (*http://www.wikipedia.com*) and find a topic that is well-known to you. Read the entry and see if, to your knowledge, there is any incorrect information. If you find incorrect information, correct it. If you do not find any incorrect information, contribute something new to the entry.

8. Go to *http://www.encyclopedia.com* and look up Elizabeth I. In what year did she die? When was she queen?

   When was the German Democratic Republic (East Germany) founded? When did the Berlin Wall come down?

9. Go to *Lonely Planet* and pretend that you are going on your ideal vacation. Research several locations before deciding where you want to go. *Money is no object!*

   – Where are you going and how long are you going to stay?

   – Find a hotel. Where are you going to stay?

   – Find and describe at least one sightseeing activity.

10. Go to *http://www.opensourceshakespeare.org/concordance/*:

    – Using 'Search Texts,' do a search for the phrase 'time is out of joint.' In what play was it used and who said it?

    – Do another search for the phrase 'There is money. Spend it; spend it; spend more.' In what play was it used and who said it?

    – Click on 'Concordance' and choose the letter 'B.' How many times was the word 'beast' used in Shakespeare's plays?

11. Go to the Internet Movie Database (*http://www.imdb.com*) and do a search for Helen Mirren. What is her birth name? In how many movies has she appeared as an actress? Name one film that she directed.

    – Look up one of your favorite actors or actresses.

    – Who is he/she? In how many movies has he/she acted?

12. Do an online search for one of your favorite musical groups and the word 'discography.' How many results came up?

    – Look at three or four of these sites.

    – Which one did you like the best and why?

Exercise 3

1. What is the Dewey classification number of your major field of interest? What is the Library of Congress classification number of your major field of interest?

2. Go to your OPAC (library catalog) and do a simple search. Find three book titles which relate to a scholarly topic such as information literacy or civil rights: list the title, author, and classification number of each.

3. Stay in the library catalog and look for an advanced search option. Search a scholarly subject of interest such as civil rights for items in various types or formats. List item titles and type or format for three different types of items, such as a reference book, audio-recording, DVD, e-book, thesis, dissertation, or other archival material.

4. Find the general classification in either Dewey or Library of Congress for the following titles:

    – *Encyclopedia of the American Constitution*

    – *Web of Deception: Misinformation on the Internet*

    – *Walden*

    – *The Iliad*

    – *Gulliver's Travels*

Additional sources

'Great Reference Books Online,' by Bartleby.com:
http://www.bartleby.com/reference/

'Identifying Primary, Secondary, and Tertiary Sources,' by UNCW Randall Library:
http://www.lib.auburn.edu/bi/typesofsources.htm

'What are Primary Sources?' by the Library of Congress:
http://memory.loc.gov/learn/lessons/psources/source.html

Notes

1. Lois Mai Chan (1994) *Cataloguing and Classification: An Introduction.* Lanham, MD: Scarecrow Press.
2. Simon Winchester (1999) *The Professor and the Madman: A Tale of Murder, Insanity, and the Making of the OED.* New York: HarperCollins.

5

Ethical literacy: scholarly communication and the academic code of conduct

A nation's treasure is in its scholars. (Old Chinese proverb)

Scholarly communication

Scholarly communication, or communication between and among researchers and other experts in a given field, may be considered *primary source information* if it is original communication or research. Scholarly communication may be formal or informal:

- Formal communication, e.g.
  - peer-reviewed scholarly journal articles, juried conference papers;
  - scholarly books;
  - specialized encyclopedia articles signed by a scholar or scholars.
- Informal communication, e.g.
  - communication by phone, e-mail, regular mail;
  - word of mouth, interaction at professional or scholarly conferences.

What is the 'invisible college'?

The term 'invisible college' was first used to describe the British Royal Society, a group of scholars and academics dating back to 1660 who met regularly to exchange research and ideas. In the 1960s, sociologist

Derek Price[1] revived the term to describe the informal communities of scholars and professionals who communicate and share research and ideas.

In 1972, Diana Crane wrote *Invisible Colleges: Diffusion of Knowledge in Scientific Communities*,[2] which explores the way social structures and scholarly communication influence the development of ideas. According to Crane, participation in an invisible college inspires a sense of purpose and focuses interest on particular issues. Members of an invisible college see themselves as part of a complex national, even global, network.

Scholarly publication cycle

After scholars have communicated informally with colleagues via the invisible college and performed literature searches of previous, related scholarly research, they develop a *research design* for a specific research project. Original research builds upon and extends previous research and thus builds the body of research in a particular field.

When the project is complete, the scholar may communicate the research results at a *professional conference*, and/or publish the article in a refereed, *peer-reviewed journal*.

The process of peer-review is a rigorous one. *Refereed or peer-reviewed journals* have editorial boards or outside expert reviewers who carefully sift articles submitted to them and judge them by exacting standards, such as soundness of research methodology, quality of writing and presentation, and originality of ideas. The reviewers exercise a gatekeeping function, that is they control what gets published according to their view of what is valuable or appropriate to their discipline or subdiscipline at the time. This process of 'quality control' is exercised by colleagues or other people in the same field and is therefore called *peer review*.

To ensure an objective review of the research, the process is usually double-blind: if the editor believes the research paper is suitable for the focus of the journal, copies with the name(s) of the author(s) removed are sent to the reviewers. The reviewers (usually three reviewers who are experts in that subject) are not known to the author(s). The reviewers may recommend: (1) accept the article for publication as is; (2) reject the article as unsuitable for publication; or (3) accept for publication with recommended revisions. The editor compiles the reviewers' remarks, summarizes them, sends them to the author(s), and oversees the requested revisions and final editing if recommended for publication. This process is a long one and may take from six months to two years between the time an article is submitted for publication and the time it appears in print. Original, peer-reviewed research is a *primary source* of information.

If the original research article is of particular importance or of widespread interest, its results may be discussed in a *monograph* (monograph, literally meaning 'one writing,' is a scholarly term for 'book').

Finally, perhaps years later, the results may be mentioned in an encyclopedia, textbook, or magazine (secondary source), and the topic listed in indexes, abstracts, and bibliographies (tertiary sources or finding aids).

This cyclic pattern of original research followed by a chain of various publication formats is known as the *publication cycle*. There are, of course, variations on the basic pattern that reflect the differing fields of study.

How can one distinguish between scholarly journals and popular magazines?

A scholarly or academic journal usually states in the journal information that it is peer-reviewed or refereed by subject experts. The purpose of a scholarly academic journal is to present current research in that field and it is usually published by a scholarly organization. In appearance, scholarly journals are less 'slick' and have few advertisements. The main or feature articles in a scholarly journal are original research and are considered *primary source* information.

Magazines

- Purpose is to sell advertising and make a profit.
- Edited, with articles that appeal to popular tastes.
- Contains many slick advertisements.
- Feature articles have few if any bibliographic references.

Professional journals

- Purpose is to promote standards and best practices in a particular profession.

- Edited, with best-practice articles that are not original research.
- Contains some advertisements that are related to a particular profession.
- Feature articles have few bibliographic references.

Scholarly, peer-reviewed journals

- Purpose is to promote and disseminate scholarly research.
- Edited; feature articles are peer-reviewed, research articles.
- Contains few if any advertisements.
- Feature or research articles have many scholarly bibliographic references.

Accreditation and the academic code of conduct

Be honorable yourself if you wish to associate with honorable people. (Old Welsh proverb)

Academia is built on the development of educational standards and the process of *peer-review* to determine if those standards are met – at the university level, the faculty level, and often the college and department level.

University accreditation

In the United Kingdom, institutions of independent further and higher education may be accredited by the British Accreditation Council (BAC – *http://www.the-bac.org/*). In 2008, the Research Assessment Exercise (RAE – *http://www.rae.ac.uk/*) evaluated the research quality of all academic disciplines based on that discipline's standards in order to produce quality profiles of research activity in institutions of higher education.

American universities are accredited by regional reviewing bodies such as the Southern Association of Colleges and Schools (SACS), whose Commission on Colleges is composed of other academics. The accrediting process requires that the university enforce certain quality standards and produce documentation of enforcement and assessment of those standards.[3]

According to the SACS *Principles of Accreditation: Foundations for Quality Enhancement* (2001):

> Accreditation by the Commission on Colleges signifies that an institution has a purpose appropriate to higher education and has resources, programs, and services sufficient to accomplish and sustain that purpose. Accreditation indicates that an institution maintains clearly specified educational objectives that are consistent with its mission and appropriate to the degrees it offers, and that it is successful in achieving its stated objectives.
>
> Both a process and a product, accreditation relies on integrity, thoughtful and principled judgment, rigorous application of requirements, and a context of trust. It provides an assessment of an institution's effectiveness in the fulfillment of its mission, its compliance with the requirements of its accrediting association, and its continuing efforts to enhance the quality of student learning and its programs and services. Based upon reasoned judgment, the process stimulates evaluation and improvement, while providing a means of continuing accountability to constituents and the public.
>
> The Commission on Colleges supports the right of an institution to pursue its established educational mission; the right of faculty members to teach, investigate, and publish freely; and the right of students to access opportunities for learning and for the open exchange of ideas. However, the exercise of these rights should not interfere with the overriding obligation of an institution to offer its students a sound education.[4]

Another organization that evaluates and rates universities is the Carnegie Foundation. Its highest rating is Doctoral/Research Universities – Extensive. Institutions with that rating typically offer a wide range of baccalaureate programs and are committed to graduate education through the doctorate (they award 50 or more doctoral degrees per year across at least 15 disciplines).[5]

College and department accreditation

In addition to the university level, many colleges within a university are accredited. For example, in the United States, a college of education may be accredited by the National Council of Accreditation for Teacher Education (NCATE – *http://www.ncate.org/*).

Some departments or programs within a college may also be accredited. In the US, library and information science (LIS) programs may be accredited by the American Library Association (ALA – *http:// www.ala.org/*). In the UK, the Chartered Institute of Library and Information Professionals (CILIP) accredits LIS programs and a qualifying scheme for advanced certification of individual practitioners.[6]

Faculty tenure and review

Faculty of academic institutions in the United Kingdom have a three-year probationary period before being considered permanent.[7] In the US, most colleges and universities use the tenure and promotion process.

Tenure, or the status of holding a position, is from the Latin *tenere* meaning 'to hold' and in academia has two main purposes:

- to promote academic freedom by reducing the fear of being fired for openly disagreeing with the authorities or popular opinion;
- to promote the production of higher quality output (research and instruction).[8]

Most faculty undergo an annual review, which includes present accomplishment and future plans and goals. Faculty tenure takes about five or six years and must be approved by other faculty, their department chair, the college dean, and the president of the university. The tenure and review process requires documentation of:

- *Teaching activity* – courses taught, number of students in each course, course evaluations, mentored students' projects, awards/honors;
- *Research and publication activity* – research projects, publication of research in scholarly peer-reviewed journals, presentation of research at conferences, authorship of books or book chapters;
- *Grant activity* – research grants, technology grants;
- *Service activity* – service to the university and college (usually by committee work), service to the department, and service to the community.

Academic code of conduct

Academic faculty and students are required to follow an ethical code of academic conduct, the basics of which are mutual respect, honesty, and integrity. Students have the right to expect fair and ethical treatment from faculty.

In addition to these rights, students have responsibilities that are usually detailed in a student handbook:

- Attend class regularly – be on time and attentive. Semesters are short and each class is important.

- Treat faculty and other students with respect both on campus and in cyberspace. Harassment is not tolerated in an academic environment and flaming (abusive language) is not tolerated in an online environment.

- Be mindful that e-mail, online chats, and text-messaging are useful but not secure. Messages in electronic format are easily forwarded, frequently archived, and should be considered part of the public record.

- Adhere to the principles of academic honesty. The work one does at a university should be one's own and many universities now use software such as turnitin.com to check for plagiarism (copying another's work and presenting it as one's own).

Copyright and plagiarism

According to the definition of copyright in the *Online Dictionary of Library and Information Science (ODLIS)*:

> The exclusive legal rights granted by a government to an author, editor, compiler, composer, playwright, publisher, or distributor to publish, produce, sell, or distribute copies of a literary, musical, dramatic, artistic, or other work, within certain limitations (*fair use* and first sale). Copyright law also governs the right to prepare derivative works, reproduce a work or portions of it, and display or perform a work in public.
>
> Such rights may be transferred or sold to others and do not necessarily pass with ownership of the work itself. Copyright protects a work in the specific form in which it is created, not the idea, theme, or concept expressed in the work, which other writers are free to interpret in a different way. A work never copyrighted or no longer protected by copyright is said to be in the *public domain*.

In 1710, the first copyright law in England gave protection to the author for 14 years, renewable for a second period of equal length. In the United States, the first federal copyright law, passed in 1790, also provided protection for 14 years, renewable for an additional 14 years if the author survived the first term. Congress extended the term in 1831 and 1909 then changed the duration of copyright to life of the author plus 50 years, effective January 1, 1978. In 1998, the controversial *Copyright Term Extension Act* (*CTEA*) lengthened the period to life of the author plus 70 years for works published on or after January 1, 1978, the same as in Europe. For anonymous works, pseudonymous works, and works for hire the period is 95 years from year of first publication or 120 years from year of creation, whichever expires first ... International copyright is governed by the *Berne Convention* and the *Universal Copyright Convention*.[9]

Fair use and fair dealing

Fair use is defined by the *ODLIS* as 'conditions under which copying a work, or a portion of it, does *not* constitute infringement of copyright, including copying for purposes of criticism, comment, news reporting, teaching, scholarship, and research.' According to the US Copyright Act, section 107 contains a list of the various purposes for which the reproduction of a particular work may be considered fair, such as criticism, comment, news reporting, teaching, scholarship, and research. Section 107 also sets out four factors to be considered in determining whether or not a particular use is fair:

- the purpose and character of the use, including whether such use is of a commercial nature or is for non-profit educational purposes;
- the nature of the copyrighted work;
- the amount and substantiality of the portion used in relation to the copyrighted work as a whole;
- the effect of the use upon the potential market for, or value of, the copyrighted work.[10]

UK copyright law states exceptions. *Fair dealing* is a term used to describe acts which are permitted to a certain degree without infringing the work. These acts are:

- private and research study purposes;
- performance, copies or lending for educational purposes;
- criticism and news reporting;
- incidental inclusion;
- copies and lending by librarians.
- acts for the purposes of royal commissions, statutory inquiries, judicial proceedings and parliamentary purposes;
- recording of broadcasts for the purposes of listening to or viewing at a more convenient time – this is known as time shifting;
- producing a back-up copy for personal use of a computer program;
- playing a sound recording for a non-profit-making organization, club or society.[11]

The *1961Report of the Register of Copyrights on the General Revision of the US Copyright Law* cites examples of fair use activities as:

> quotation of excerpts in a review or criticism for purposes of illustration or comment; quotation of short passages in a scholarly or technical work, for illustration or clarification of the author's observations; use in a parody of some of the content of the work parodied; summary of an address or article, with brief quotations, in a news report; reproduction by a library of a portion of a work to replace part of a damaged copy; reproduction by a teacher or student of a small part of a work to illustrate a lesson; reproduction of a work in legislative or judicial proceedings or reports; incidental and fortuitous reproduction, in a newsreel or broadcast, of a work located in the scene of an event being reported.[12]

Academic honesty and plagiarism

Plagiarism is commonly associated with cheating. However, most plagiarism is not the result of cheating. Rather, it is the result of a lack of knowledge of how to properly document a source and how to distinguish between what information is borrowed from another source and that which is original to you, the author. While this lack of knowledge of how to cite sources properly is still plagiarism, it is called unintentional plagiarism and is not as serious an offense as deliberately stealing information from another source.[13]

Consider the following paragraph:

> In 'Real Old Time T'ing,' code-switching from Jamaican Creole to Jamaican Standard English is done for the following four reasons: (1) to reflect Patricia's change in social class; (2) to reflect Papa Sterling's need to convey his higher status as a parent to his daughter Patricia; (3) to make fun of Patricia's middle-class ideas that a bigger home is a better home; and (4) to reflect the element of formality involved in speech-making.

The above paragraph is obviously plagiarized because no source and no page numbers were given. However, what if the paragraph were rewritten in the following way:

> In 'Real Old Time T'ing,' the characters code-switch from Jamaican Creole to Jamaican Standard English for the following reasons: (1) to note Patricia's change in status from lower to middle class; (2) to reflect Papa Sterling's need to convey to his daughter his higher status as her father; (3) to make fun of Patricia's new middle-class ideas of a larger home being the best home; and (4) to convey the element of formality involved in making a speech.

Is the above paragraph plagiarized? Yes, it definitely is. The above paragraph still maintains much of the sentence structure and vocabulary of the original, with only minor changes made. Would it be plagiarism if you put (Wright, 1993) after it? Yes, it would. As aforementioned, the paragraph maintains much of the structure and vocabulary of the original. Thus, for it not to be plagiarism, the author's last name, year of publication, and page number would need to be included. In addition, either quotation marks or a block quotation format (indenting the paragraph five spaces from the left margin) would need to be used when formatting quotations using the *Publication Manual of the American Psychological Association*. Since the above paragraph is over 40 words, a block quotation format is needed:[14]

> In 'Real Old Time T'ing,' the characters code-switch from Jamaican Creole to Jamaican Standard English for the following reasons: (1) to note Patricia's change in status from lower to middle class; (2) to reflect Papa Sterling's need to convey to his daughter his higher status as her father; (3) to make fun of Patricia's new middle-class ideas of a larger home being the best home; and (4) to convey the element of formality involved in making a speech. (Wright, 1993: 25)

If the paragraph were rewritten in the following way, would it be plagiarism?

> In 'Real Old Time T'ing,' Papa Sterling goes from using Jamaican Creole to Jamaican Standard English in order to convey to his daughter that he is the parent, to make fun of his daughter's new fancy ideas, and to make a speech. His daughter Patricia code-switches to reflect her rise from the lower to the middle class.

As the above paragraph is written, it would be plagiarism because there is no citation. While the paragraph has been successfully paraphrased, a citation needs to be included in order to give credit for the author's ideas. Citing the paragraph as follows would make it acceptable and not plagiarized:

> In 'Real Old Time T'ing,' Papa Sterling goes from using Jamaican Creole to Jamaican Standard English in order to convey to his daughter that he is the parent, to make fun of his daughter's new fancy ideas, and to make a speech. His daughter Patricia code-switches to reflect her rise from the lower to the middle class. (Wright, 1993)[15]

No page number is needed because the paragraph is not a direct quote. Thus credit only needs to be given for the author's ideas and not for her words.

Paraphrasing may be defined as using another person's ideas and rewriting them in your own words. It differs from summarizing in that a summary is generally a shortened version of a paragraph or passage in which only the main ideas are given. A paraphrase, however, is generally the rewriting of the entire paragraph or passage in your own words.

How to successfully paraphrase

1. Read the material in the original source carefully.
2. Read the material again and take notes on the content.
3. Put the material down for several hours.
4. After several hours, return to your notes and compose them for your paper.
5. Compare what you have written to the original source. Make any changes in vocabulary and sentence structure which are too close to that of the original.

6. The most important thing to remember about paraphrasing is that you are borrowing someone else's ideas but not their words. The words are your own, while ideas belong to someone else.

How to avoid plagiarism in academic writing

1. Always keep copies of your original sources with you. This will make it easier to cite your sources as you are writing your paper.

2. Cite any quotation from another source unless it is common knowledge (e.g. Shakespeare was born in Stratford-upon-Avon, or Albany is the capital of New York State).

3. You must cite quoted and paraphrased material in both the text and in the reference list at the end.

4. You must cite paraphrased material. With quotations, you cite to give another author credit for using his/her *words*. In paraphrasing, you cite to give another credit for using his/her *ideas* in your work.[16]

Exercises

Exercise 1

1. Look up your school, college, or university's code of academic conduct. What are the main points? What are the consequences for plagiarism?

Exercise 2

1. Read the following two paragraphs and successfully paraphrase them.

   (a) Socialization occurs when a newcomer is made a member of the community and begins to adhere to the norms of the group. Norms are important for understanding the process of socialization because they act as rules and provide the standards for regulation of individual and group behavior (Hawkes, 1975). In particular, graduate school socialization is the process whereby students gain the knowledge, skills, and values necessary for entry into a professional career that requires advanced or specialized knowledge and/or skill. Socialization of graduate students occurs through classroom learning, relationships with faculty and peers, and involvement in the life of the department and the larger professional community (Weidman, Twale, and Stein, 2001). Doctoral programs typically involve a somewhat lengthy process of adult socialization in cognitive skills, appropriate attitudes toward research and scholarship, and other field specific values (Clark and Corcoran, 1986) (as cited in Gentry and Wright, 2009).[17]

(b) Critical theory is a social theory whose major component is to 'critique and change the whole of society' rather than to explain societal phenomena (Hill, 2007).[18] According to critical theory, problems such as low literacy, lack of education, and inequality in salaries or employment opportunities are the result of certain societal systems maintaining all of the power and oppressing those who are not of the same socio-economic class. Societal systems are those such as the government or the educational system. The goal of these societal systems is to maintain the status quo and the existing social class structure. The goal of critical theory is to create an awareness of the oppression and inequality in society. Once this awareness has been created, those who are not part of the system will hopefully begin to resist societal inequalities and work to create change. Knowledge is power; knowledge is emancipatory, then, and once knowledge has been gained, those not in power can work to create a more equitable society. The goal of learning should be to create change by creating awareness of and raising people's consciousness of societal ills and issues.

Exercise 3

Look at the following paragraphs and then look at the paraphrased paragraphs below each. Determine if the material is successfully paraphrased or plagiarized. If the paragraph is plagiarized, rewrite it to successfully paraphrase it.

1. *Original paragraph*:

   People who are keen observers of social settings and other people tend to make good qualitative researchers. Do you want to know how things are done in unfamiliar settings or occupations? Are you a people watcher? Do you notice what other people wear? How they speak and behave? Can you guess how they might be feeling? Do you pay attention to who speaks first, who replies to whom, and how people respond in a conversation? Do you naturally ask questions that begin with how, what, why? People who do this are often able to perceive things in situations that others may not ... Qualitative research is based on a holistic world view, where people's perceptions have meaning within given contexts. (Hill, 2007: 27)[19]

Paraphrase:

People who are astute observers of their social surroundings and others generally make really good researchers. Do you have an interest in the workings of unfamiliar settings, jobs, and people and their clothing? Do you pay attention to people's feelings, to who speaks first in a conversation, how they respond? Do you ask a lot of how, what, and why questions? People who do this are likely to be more perceptive than those who do not.

2. *Original paragraph*:

Qualitative research is process-oriented and takes time. Trying to hurry will short-change the process and diminish the results. It is bad practice to begin a qualitiative research project by trying to predict the study's timeline or findings. Researchers cannot do justice to a long-term study if they try to minimize the time spent in data collection and analysis. Researchers need to have patience and persistence with the process, enjoy it, and follow it all the way through. As a novice researcher, you will make missteps or realize that you want to approach an issue differently as your study evolves. This happens to experienced researchers, too ... (Hill, 2007: 29)[20]

Paraphrase:

Qualitative research requires a process-oriented approach and takes a lot of time. Trying to hurry the process along will diminish the results. It is not good practice to start your qualitative research paper by trying to predict the length of the study or the final results. Researchers cannot do a long-term study justice if they try to cut corners in data collection and analysis. Researchers need to be patient and persistent throughout the process, enjoy what they are doing, and see it through to the end. As a new researcher, you will make mistakes and realize that you want to change things all through the process. This happens to experienced researchers as well.

3. *Original paragraph*:

Can you talk to other people and let them lead the conversation? Watch an interview done on a morning news show and see how many interviewers appear to actually supply the interviewee's answers. 'That must have been awful!' they'll say, which leaves the person with little response but to say yes. In a qualitative interview, the researcher's interviewing skills bring a calming effect, which allows the participant to be at ease and speak freely. A researcher asks questions that get others talking, follows their lead, and lets them introduce new topics. The researcher may have come prepared with an interview guide, but will let the other person lead the conversation. Sometimes people need to take a breather if they are talking about a difficult experience; allowing them to talk about something else for a little while serves this purpose. A good interview is one characterized by the fact the interviewer's voice is heard very little. (Hill, 2007: 28)[21]

Paraphrase:

Can you allow others to take charge of the dialogue in conversation? Are you able to watch an interview on television and critique the interviewer? Do you notice if the interviewer allows the interviewee to answer his/her questions or does he/she supply the answer and 'force' the interviewee to agree with the interviewer? In a qualitative research interview, the interviewer should be able to put the interviewee at ease so that he/she will be able to speak openly. The interviewer's questions should be open-ended so that they allow interviewees to take the discussion in whatever direction they choose. In other words, even though the interviewer may have pre-set questions, the interviewee actually guides the conversation. If the topic of discussion is an emotional one such as the death of a family member or sexual abuse, the interviewee may need to take breaks during the interview or to change the conversation to a more neutral topic for a while. The mark of a good interview is how infrequently the interviewer speaks. (Hill, 2007: 28)[22]

Additional sources

Copyright Clearance Center:
http://www.copyright.com/

'Copyright & Fair Use Overview,' by Stanford University Libraries:
http://fairuse.stanford.edu/Copyright_and_Fair_Use_Overview/
'Copyright & Fair Use in the Classroom, on the Internet, & the WWW,'
by University of Maryland University College:
http://www.umuc.edu/library/copy.shtml
Fair Use Simply Explained:
http://www.thecopyrightsite.org/fairuse.html
Harvard University Academic Code of Conduct:
http://www.hks.harvard.edu/degrees/registrar/procedures/conduct
Netiquette:
http://www.albion.com/netiquette/corerules.html
'What Is Academic Discourse?' Washington State University Libraries
Tutorial:
*http://www.wsulibs.wsu.edu/electric/trainingmods/Gened300/academic_
disciplines/discourse.htm*

Notes

1. Derek J. de Solla Price (1963) *Little Science, Big Science*. New York: Columbia University Press; Derek J. de Solla Price and Donald Beaver (1966) 'Collaboration in an invisible college,' *American Psychologist*, 21(1): 1101–17.
2. Diana Crane (1972) *Invisible Colleges: Diffusion of Knowledge in Scientific Communities*. Chicago: University of Chicago Press.
3. Southern Association of Colleges and Schools, Commission on Colleges (n.d.) 'General Information on the Accreditation Process,' at: *http://www.sacscoc.org/genaccproc.asp* (accessed 7 July 2007).
4. Southern Association of Colleges and Schools, Commission on Colleges (2001) *Principles of Accreditation: Foundations for Quality Enhancement*. SACS. Online at: *http://www.sacscoc.org/pdf/PrinciplesOfAccreditation.PDF* (accessed 7 July 2007).
5. University of Washington (n.d.) 'Carnegie Doctoral/Research Universities – Extensive,' at: *http://www.washington.edu/tools/universities.html* (accessed 9 July 2008).
6. Kendra S. Albright and Robert A. Petrulis (2007) 'Academic life of information scholars: cross-cultural comparisons of the United States and England,' *Bulletin of the American Society for Information Science and Technology*, 33(4): 27–8.
7. Ibid.
8. Susan E. Higgins and Teresa S. Welsh (2009) 'The tenure process in LIS: a survey of LIS/IS program directors,' *Journal of Education for Library and Information Science (JELIS)*, 50(3): 176–89.

9. Joan M. Reitz (n.d.) *ODLIS – Online Dictionary for Library and Information Science*, at: *http://lu.com/odlis/odlis_c.cfm#copyright* (accessed 3 May 2009).
10. US Copyright Office (n.d.) 'Fair Use Fact Sheet,' at: *http://www.copyright.gov/fls/fl102.html* (accessed 5 September 2009).
11. UK Copyright Service (n.d.) 'UK Copyright Law Fact Sheet P-01,' at: *http://www.copyrightservice.co.uk/copyright/p01_uk_copyright_law* (accessed 5 September 2009).
12. *Register's Report on the General Revision of the U.S. Copyright Law*, 1961, at: *http://www.ipmall.info/hosted_resources/lipa/copyrights/SUMMARY%20OF%20RECOMMENDATIONS.pdf* (accessed 7 September 2009).
13. John Rachal (2009) *REF 889: The Dissertation Process*. Course Manual. Hattiesburg, MS: University of Southern Mississippi.
14. Authors' note: Information about the block quotations and the format of the paragraph is written according to the guides of the *Publication Manual of the American Psychological Association*, 5th edn. Other style guides may format longer quotations differently. Please check your style guide when formatting longer quotations.
15. Melissa Wright (1993) 'Code-Switching in Jamaican Literature,' Linguistics 620 class paper, p. 25. Bloomington, IN: Indiana University.
16. John Rachal (2009) *REF 889: The Dissertation Process*. Course Manual. Hattiesburg, MS: University of Southern Mississippi.
17. Roland K. Hawkes (1975) 'Norms, deviance, and social control: a mathematical elaboration of concepts,' *American Journal of Sociology*, 80: 886–908; John Weidman, Darla Twale, and Elizabeth Stein (2001) 'Socialization of graduate and professional students in higher education: a perilous passage?' *ASHE ERIC Higher Education Report*, 28(3): 1–100; Shirley M. Clark and Mary Corcoran (1986) 'Perspectives on the professional socialization of women faculty: a case of accumulative disadvantage,' *Journal of Higher Education*, 57: 20–43, cited in Deb Gentry and Melissa Wright (2009) 'Thrown to the Wolves: The Socialization Experiences of Female Doctoral Students,' unpublished manuscript.
18. Lillian Hill (2007) 'Thoughts for students considering becoming qualitative researchers: qualities of qualitative researchers,' *Qualitative Research Journal*, 7(1): 26–31.
19. Ibid., p. 27.
20. Ibid., p. 29.
21. Ibid., p. 28.
22. Ibid.

6

Network literacy: database searching

Knowledge is of two kinds. We know a subject ourselves, or we know where we can find information on it. (Samuel Johnson)

What is a database?

Data are raw facts. A database is a collection of digital items, a 'large, regularly updated file of digitized information.'[1]

The two most common types of databases are bibliographic and full-text:

- A *bibliographic database* contains electronic entries called records containing a uniform description of a specific document, usually retrievable by author, title, subject heading (descriptor), or keyword(s), and usually containing citations and abstracts or summaries of the documents. A good example of a bibliographic database is a library's OPAC (online public access catalog). For each book or other item in the database, the following information is generally included in the OPAC record: title, author, copyright date, card catalog number, and subject.

- A *full-text database* provides the entire text of single works, such as journal articles (definitions taken from *ODLIS*).[2] Full-text databases include *Academic Search Premier*, *Literary Reference Center*, and *JSTOR*. Most online databases with full-text availability have full-text articles dating back about 20 years.

These categories are somewhat overlapping – a bibliographic database may contain some full-text documents, while some supposedly full-text databases may not contain complete texts of every document in them.

Most items in a database contain some descriptive information. At the Royal Society Scientific Information Conference in 1948, they established two important needs at that time: (1) that research papers need author abstracts (descriptive paragraphs); and (2) that there is a need to know how scientists gather their information so that it can be organized more effectively.[3]

In addition to being categorized as bibliographic or full-text, a database may also be either *general* or *subject-specific*. One example of a general academic database is *Academic Search Premier*, which contains bibliographic citations and selected full-text articles for popular newspapers and magazines as well as scholarly journals in nearly every academic discipline dating back as far as 1965.

Two examples of subject-specific databases are *Library Literature and Information Science Full Text* and *Medline*, the latter containing citations to biomedical articles from journals in such fields as medicine, nursing, dentistry, veterinary medicine, and health care systems.

How does one search a database?

Choosing a database

The first step in using a database is identifying an appropriate database to use. In searching for information for a research paper, one may wish to begin with a scholarly reference source such as *Credo Reference Books Online* (*http://www.credoreference.com*), *History Reference Center*, or *Literary Reference Center* for general background information on a topic for the paper introduction.

It is then appropriate to use either a large general database such as *Academic Search Premier* or a subject-specific database such as *Communication and Mass Media Complete*. Some vendors or aggregators of multiple databases, such as EBSCOhost (*http://www .ebscohost.com/*), allow a search of multiple databases.

Limiting a search

Most academic databases allow one to limit searches in several ways:

- by format, such as newspapers, journal articles, book reviews, images;
- by date;

- by availability in full-text;
- by search field:
  - a basic search or keyword search will search all the fields in a database;
  - an advanced search allows one to search in specific fields such as author, subject, title.

To find scholarly, primary source research articles, limit the search to 'peer-reviewed' and 'feature article' and/or 'references available' if those options are available.

To narrow a search to find fewer but more relevant items, search in specific fields. For instance, try searching for a relevant word or term in the subject field or the abstract field.

Effective search strategies: using Boolean

One of the most powerful parts of electronic versions of information resources is the ability to search for complex subjects by combining words and concepts using something called *Boolean logic*. Boolean logic is named after nineteenth-century British mathematician George Boole who invented Boolean algebra.[4]

The three major *Boolean* or *logical operators* used in information retrieval are:

- AND
- OR
- NOT

AND is used to combine concepts – by adding more restrictions to search criteria, it *narrows* the number of hits (items retrieved):

- Both concepts must be present in the retrieved document.
- Limits, restricts set size.
- The more one uses AND, the fewer items one retrieves.

For example, if you do a search for bipolar disorder on *Academic Search Premier*, when you type in *bipolar disorder*, you obtain over 7,200 results, way too many for any one researcher to manage.

However, if you do another search with the following terms, *bipolar disorder AND children*, the number of results obtained is over 1,000 – much better but still very difficult to manage.

If you do another search with the following terms, *bipolar disorder AND children AND treatment*, over 400 results are obtained – once again, much better, but still far too many for a single researcher or a single paper.

A final search, however, using the terms *bipolar disorder AND children AND treatment AND psychotherapy*, results in 27 'hits.' The 27 hits are manageable and can be easily sorted through to choose the right sources.

AND narrows your search by including only results with *all* of your search terms in them. For example, a search string of *bipolar disorder AND children* returns only results in which both terms – bipolar disorder and children – appear. A search string of *bipolar disorder AND children AND treatment AND psychotherapy* returns only those results in which all four terms – bipolar disorder, children, treatment, and psychotherapy – appear in the article.

OR *broadens or expands* a search, or retrieves more items by including in the search either each term used or all terms used.

- Synonyms (nuclear OR atomic). Returns searches with the following terms: atomic, nuclear, or both atomic and nuclear.

- Instances/examples (Southeast OR Tennessee OR Mississippi). Returns searches with the following terms:
  - Southeast
  - Tennessee
  - Mississippi
  - Southeast and Tennessee
  - Southeast and Mississippi
  - Tennessee and Mississippi
  - Southeast, Tennessee, and Mississippi.

- Antonyms (water quality OR water pollution; safety OR hazard). A search of water quality OR water pollution returns searches with the following terms:
  - water quality
  - water pollution
  - water quality and water pollution.

- Alternative terms (hurricanes OR tornadoes; computers OR automation). A search of hurricanes OR tornadoes returns searches with the following terms:

- hurricanes
- tornadoes
- hurricanes and tornadoes.

NOT *excludes* documents, restricting set size (a set is a list or group of items retrieved in a particular database search). Thus NOT narrows your search results by omitting terms. For example, the search string *hurricanes NOT football team NOT drink* excludes references to the Miami Hurricanes football team and the drink, Hurricane, which is commonly served in New Orleans.

■ Use with caution – may exclude relevant documents.

Nesting

One may use any combination of logical operators in a single search. Parentheses are used to specify the correct order of processing (search terms inside parentheses are executed first). Nesting is recommended if your search statement includes three or more terms. For example:

■ smoking AND (adolescents OR teenagers)

■ (smoking OR tobacco OR nicotine) AND (adolescents OR teenagers)

■ (mathematics OR arithmetic) AND (formula OR algorithm)

Effective search strategies: using wildcard and truncation

Using a wildcard or truncation symbol *expands* a search by retrieving articles that are related to a root stem:

■ Wildcard substitutes a symbol within a word. For instance, if the wildcard symbol is '?', wom?n will retrieve items with 'woman' and 'women.'

■ Truncation is the addition of a symbol at the beginning or end of a word stem to retrieve items related to variations of that term. 'Truncation is particularly useful in retrieving both the singular and the plural forms of a word in the same search,'[5] for example librar* to retrieve articles containing 'librarian,' 'librariana,' 'librarianship,' 'libraries,' etc.

In most online catalogs and bibliographic databases, the truncation symbol is the * (asterisk), but since the wildcard and truncation symbols are not standardized, other symbols may be used (?, $, #, +).

To find what wildcard and truncation symbols are used in a particular database, click on 'help' or the '?' symbol.

Effective search strategies: using a bound phrase

Using a bound phrase *narrows* a search to words or terms in a specific order. Most commonly, one can search for a bound phrase by enclosing the desired term or phrase in quotation marks, such as 'Abraham Lincoln' or 'America the Beautiful.'

Other database features

The trend is for databases to contain more full-text materials and more multimedia.

- One useful feature is the ability to select and save article citations in a folder, then print or e-mail the citation (as well as the full-text article if available) to the user in the citation style of choice.

- Other useful features include the availability of features such as a literary timeline in the *Literary Reference Center* database or video clips in the *History Reference Center* database.

Evaluating information sources

How can one evaluate information sources?

In order to evaluate information resources, one must determine what information is needed and for what purpose.

In an academic setting, the most common need is for information sources for a scholarly paper. For that purpose, a variety of resources is usually required, depending on the topic:

- Reference works, such as a dictionary or subject encyclopedia, are useful to find background information for a paper's introduction.

- Primary sources, either original, first-person (archival) sources or original research (peer-reviewed scholarly journal articles), are the most reliable sources to use for a scholarly paper.

- Websites, if their use is permitted, should be those that go through a process of review and recommendation, such as those archived in the *Internet Scout Project* (*scout.wisc.edu/Archives/*) – do not use Wikipedia sources in a scholarly paper.

- Scholarly books, considered secondary sources, should be those that have been authored by an expert knowledgeable in their field.

- Newspapers or news reports may be useful if current or eyewitness reports are needed.

- Statistics, usually available online from government sources, may be useful depending on the topic.

Criteria for evaluating information sources

- *Authority, or authorship* – who is the author of the work? Are the author's credentials credible, for example an academic faculty member or researcher or other expert in their field?

- *Date* – when was the information source published? Is the date appropriate? For instance, one may want older sources for historical background but if writing about a current topic, the most recent research or other information on that topic should be used.

- *Documentation* – does the source have a bibliography that cites previous studies or other relevant information?

- *Objectivity* – is the source unbiased and objective? Is the information presented in a non-biased manner?

Exercises

Exercise 1

Choose a very broad topic (it may be a topic for one of your research projects or a topic in which you are interested) and do a search on *Academic Search Premier* or another online database.

1. How many results did you obtain from this search?

2. Do another search where you narrow your topic by adding another term and AND (bipolar disorder AND children). How many results did you obtain?

3. Keep narrowing your search by adding terms connected by AND until you narrow your results down to 15–20. What was your final search string?

Exercise 2

1. Do a search for *mathematics activities* on one of the online databases. How many results did you obtain?

2. Do another search for *(mathematics OR arithmetic) AND activities*. How many results did you obtain?

Exercise 3

1. Choose a specific, scholarly topic. Find and list the following sources:

   - a dictionary that contains a definition of the topic;
   - an encyclopedia article related to the topic;
   - a scholarly book related to the topic;
   - a relevant peer-reviewed article from a scholarly journal;
   - a relevant, scholarly website.

Additional sources

'A Primer in Boolean Logic':
   http://www.internettutorials.net/boolean.asp
'Critical Evaluation of Resources':
   http://www.lib.berkeley.edu/instruct/guides/evaluation.html
'Critically Analyzing Information Sources':
   http://www.library.cornell.edu/olinuris/ref/research/skill26.htm
'Evaluating Information Sources: Basic Principles,' by Duke University Libraries:
   http://library.duke.edu/services/instruction/libraryguide/evaluating.html
'Evaluation Quiz':
   http://regisnet.regiscollege.edu/library/infolit/evalquiz2.htm

Notes

1. Joan Reitz, *ODLIS – Online Dictionary of Library and Information Science*, at: *http://lu.com/odlis/* (accessed 3 July 2008).
2. Ibid.
3. S. Herner (1984) 'A brief history of information science,' *Journal of the American Society for Information Science*, 38(3): 157–63.
4. Desmond MacHale (1985) *George Boole: His Life and Work*. Dublin: Boole Press.
5. Reitz, op. cit.

7

Computer literacy: computer hardware and software

A computer does not substitute for judgment any more than a pencil substitutes for literacy. But writing without a pencil is no particular advantage. (Robert McNamara)

What is a computer?

The purpose of a computer is to process data into information (data → information). A computer may be defined literally as a 'machine that computes' or as 'a machine that can be programmed to manipulate symbols. Computers can perform complex and repetitive procedures quickly, precisely and reliably and can quickly store and retrieve large amounts of data.'[1]

How did the computer develop?

Five ages of the computer

Depending on the definition and how far back in time one wishes to journey, the origins of the computer may be dated to the abacus or one of the later calculating machines listed in the timeline below.

1. *Pre-Mechanical Age* (5,000 BC to AD 1450). The abacus, a system of sliding beads on a rack, was used about 3,000 BC in Asia Minor for calculating and is still in use today.

2. *Mechanical Age* (1450–1840). The Babbage Analytical Engine, 1833, is considered the first steam-powered computer. Charles Babbage is considered by many to be the 'Father of the Computer' and his

assistant, Lady Ada Lovelace, the 'First Computer Programmer' because she wrote mathematics problems for Babbage's machines.[2]

3. *Electro-mechanical Age* (1840–1940). Punched card sorting was invented by Hollerith in 1890 to count the US census in six weeks instead of ten years. Hollerith founded the Tabulating Machine Co. in 1896 and in 1924 the company became International Business Machines (IBM).[3]

4. *Electronic Age* (1940–1990s).

5. *Information Age or Digital Age* (1990s – present).

Five generations of electronic computers

Frequently great advances in technology occur during times of war or national crisis as emergency funding is poured into research and development.

During the Second World War, a brilliant young British mathematician, Alan Turing (1912–54), was recruited as a cryptographer to work on the German Enigma code. He was instrumental in the development of Colossus, a special-purpose computer that was able to decipher the Nazi code. Colossus (aptly named with its 1,800 vacuum tubes) was one of the world's earliest working programmable electronic digital computers.[4]

1. First-generation computers (1940–56): vacuum tubes

    – Atanasoff-Berry Computer (1940) – first all-electric computer, Iowa State College.[5]

    – Colossus (1943) – designed by British mathematician Alan Turing to decipher the German Enigma Code.

    – ENIAC – Electronic Numerical Integrator and Computer (1946), University of Pennsylvania Army Research Laboratory: weighed 30 tons and had 18,000 vacuum tubes.[6]

    – UNIVAC – Universal Automatic Computer (1951), built by Remington Rand, was one of the first commercially available computers. UNIVAC successfully predicted Eisenhower would be the winner of the 1952 presidential election.[7]

2. Second-generation computers (1956–63): transistors

    – Solid-state design with transistors: printers, tape storage, disk storage, memory, stored programs.

    – Computer languages COBOL and FORTRAN developed.

- Stretch Computer by IBM and LARC (Livermore Atomic Research Computer) by Sperry-Rand, both developed in 1956 for atomic energy labs.[8]

- IBM 1401 and other commercial computers became widely used by businesses, universities, and governments in the 1960s.[9]

3. Third-generation computers (1964–71): integrated circuits

- Integrated circuits developed by Kilby at Texas Instruments contained three electronic components on a semiconductor, a very small, thin silicon disk that did not generate heat like a transistor.[10]

- Operating systems developed that allowed machines to run many different programs at once.[11]

4. Fourth-generation computers (1971 – present): microprocessors

- The Intel 4004 chip (1971) had all the components (central processing unit, memory, input and output) on a tiny chip microprocessor.

- Computers became available to consumers in the mid-1970s from Commodore, Radio Shack and Apple, with word-processing and spreadsheet programs most common.

- Video games Pac-Man and Atari became available in the early 1980s and ignited consumer interest in computers.

- The IBM PC (personal computer) introduced in 1981, Apple Macintosh in 1984.

5. Fifth-generation (present and future): artificial intelligence

- Superconductors being developed to speed flow of information.

- Digital convergence links TV, telephone, electricity, and computer through one fiber-optic cable or by satellite.

- Examples in the movies of 'artificial intelligence' – HAL 9000 from Arthur C. Clarke's *2001: A Space Odyssey*, *The Terminator*, and of course *AI*.[12]

What is the difference between computer hardware and software?

Computer *hardware* may be defined as the physical or mechanical parts of the computer:

- The *CPU* or computer processing unit is the part of the computer that contains the motherboard which processes the programming instructions. The CPU may be a separate unit, usually a large, rectangular box that also contains the disk inserts, or it may be built into the computer itself as one unit as in laptop computers and Mac computers.

- The *motherboard* is the main circuit board of the computer. It may also be referred to as the mainboard or system board. It contains the CPU, memory socket, and controller sockets for the mouse, keyboard, and disk drives, and the printer. (The CPU may be considered the brain of the computer, while the motherboard may be considered the spine.)

- *Data storage* includes built-in permanent storage (memory cards) and external storage such as an external hard drive, zip drive, CD (compact disk), or flash drive (also known as a thumb drive). Data storage may be ROM (read-only memory), which contains data that cannot be edited, or RAM (random-access memory), which allows stored data to be edited.

- *Information output devices* such as the monitor or viewing screen, speakers, and printer.

- *Information input devices* such as a mouse, keyboard, touch-screen, video camera, and modem (a device that allows data to be transmitted to and from a computer via a phone line, or cable or satellite connection).

Computer *software*, also known as computer programs or applications, are sets of instructions that are written by programmers. Software types include the following:

- *Operating systems* control the main functions of a computer. The leading operating system for personal computers (PCs) is Microsoft Windows. One alternative free (open-source) operating system is Linux (*http://www.linux.org*).

- *Drivers* allow computer devices such as the modem and printer to communicate data to the CPU.

- *Utility software* allows useful tasks to be performed that increase the efficiency of a computer, such as data compression and data recovery.

- *Application software* accomplishes specific tasks such as word processing, data spreadsheets, presentations, or photo-editing.

Some software programs and applications are built into a computer, such as the Windows operating system, and some basic utility programs, such as disk cleanup and disk defragmenter (Programs/Accessories/System Tools). There are three options for software that may be installed by the user:

- Commercial software may be purchased as a physical package, usually a compact disk (CD), or downloaded and installed from Internet sites.
- Shareware is software that may be used for free for a trial period then purchased.
- Freeware is software that is free.

Download.com has a variety of shareware and freeware software. Two sites that have a variety of free, useful applications are Zoho (*http://www.zoho.com*) and Open Office (*http://www.openoffice.org*).

Binary code

Computers read words and numbers as series of two numbers, 0 and 1. This is called *binary code*. Each letter or number inputted into the computer is read and stored by the computer as a series of 0s and 1s. Each 0 or 1 is called a *bit*, while 8 bits together are called a *byte*. Each letter or number is represented by a byte. The English alphabet is represented by the following binary code:

Letter	Code	Letter	Code
A	01000001	a	01100001
B	01000001	b	01100010
C	01000011	c	01100011
D	01000100	d	01100100
E	01000101	e	01100101
F	01000110	f	01100110
G	01000111	g	01100111
H	01001000	h	01101000
I	01001001	i	01101001
J	01001010	j	01101010
K	01001011	k	01101011
L	01001100	l	01101100
M	01001101	m	01101101
N	01001110	n	01101110
O	01001111	o	01101111

Letter	Code	Letter	Code
P	01010000	p	01110000
Q	01010001	q	01110001
R	01010010	r	01110010
S	01010011	s	01110011
T	01010100	t	01110100
U	01010101	u	01110101
V	01010110	v	01110110
W	01010111	w	01110111
X	01011000	x	01111000
Y	01011001	y	01111001
Z	01011010	z	01111010

Thus the term 'binary code' in binary code would be stored by the computer as:

```
01000010    01101001    01101110    01100001
01110010    01111001    01100011    01101111
01100100    01100101
```

Exercises

Exercise 1

1. Write out the following sentence in binary code: Using binary code can be fun.

2. Working with a partner, create a phrase in binary code and then have your partner write the phrase in English.

Exercise 2

Complete a Word tutorial (*http://office.microsoft.com/en-us/training/*) then using Microsoft Word or a similar word-processing program, complete the following exercise.

1. Change the font of this text to 16 pt Century Gothic.

2. Cut and paste the text from the previous question, and bold and center the text.

3. Run a spelling and grammar check on the following sentence, and correct the errors using the replace option:

    After the unfortunat accident with the spilled soda, Jen's kwyboard ever quit worked the same again.

4. What errors did Word miss?

5. Highlight this text in purple.

6. Create a numbered list of your top four favorite foods using the numbering feature.

7. Apply a word effect to the word 'information.'

8. Insert page numbers into this document.

9. Using the thesaurus, find suggested words to replace the word 'unique,' and list them below.

10. Insert a small picture of a flag (no more than 2 inches × 2 inches or 5 × 5 cm).

11. Change the margins of the entire document to 1.5 inches or 4 cm on all sides.

12. Insert a table consisting of 3 columns and 2 rows. Type the following words into the table in any order: Bill, Bob, Brandy, Boris, Brian, Bubbles.

13. Using the find and replace feature, replace all occurrences of the word purple with the word mauve.

14. Create a running header consisting of your name and LIS 201.

15. Take the following text and place it into two columns.

    There are no group assignments in this course. Students are expected to do their own work on all assignments, quizzes, and exams. Plagiarism or academic dishonesty will result in an F for the assignment or for the course, at the instructor's discretion.

16. Perform a word count and provide the number of words.

17. Using the sort feature, put the following in ascending alphabetical order:

    Bauble

    Gem

    Jewelry

    Rocks

    Ice

    Bling

18. Insert the copyright symbol here.

19. Using expanded spacing, type your first and last names.

20. Cut and paste your name here, and apply 'sparkle text.'[13]

Exercise 3

Create a résumé.

1. Format:

    – Either center or left align the heading with your name, address, and contact information (e-mail, phone). Your name should be larger than the rest of the text (usually 14 or 16 point font).

    – Single-space with an extra space between categories.

    – Be consistent in your heading and content format. For example, bold the heading, then indent or use a bulleted list for the content items.

    – The content items should be concise and consistent. Do not use personal pronouns and consistently begin each list item in a similar manner, for example with action verbs or nouns.

2. Content:

    – The objective category is optional. Lead with your strongest category and list items in reverse chronological order (most recent at the top).

3. Education:

    – List the degree, type of degree, institution, and year of graduation.

        ▪ You may list some relevant coursework, such as study abroad.

        ▪ You may list honor societies or list as a separate honors category.

4. Work experience:

    – List each position and date.

        ▪ You may include some major job responsibilities under this category.

5. Military experience:

    – Use this as a category, if applicable, or list under work experience.

6. Honors (or awards or accomplishments or achievements):

  - You may list honors, awards, accomplishments, or achievements as appropriate or applicable.

7. Service:

  - You may list any university, organizational, or community service, including leadership or membership in student or community organizations. This is a good time to join a group and participate in some service activities that you can list on the résumé.

    ▪ You may list any major service activities or projects.

8. References:

  - Available upon request.

Exercise 4

Complete an Excel tutorial (*http://office.microsoft.com/en-us/training/*) then, using Microsoft Excel or a similar spreadsheet program, complete the following exercise.

1. Search the Internet for information about an imaginary trip and create a budget in an Excel spreadsheet for that trip:

  - Title the spreadsheet at the bottom; label the rows.
  - Include transportation costs such as airfare, as well as lodging and estimates for meals, tours/sightseeing, and entertainment.
  - Label the cost column and format the cells in the row for currency.
  - Use a formula to calculate the total at the bottom.
  - Use your imagination – plan to go where you want, spend whatever you want.

Exercise 5

1. Use PowerPoint (or equivalent software) to prepare a slide presentation of 5–10 slides on an approved topic of interest, then present the slide presentation to a group.

    – *Presentation guidelines*

- Prepare content that is appropriate and interesting.
- Use a consistent and simple background design and font (dark text on a light background is most readable).
- Vary the presentation with bulleted lists, use of columns, and appropriate use of images or figures.
- Limit the number of words; use key phrases then edit for conciseness.
- Be consistent with items in bulleted lists, such as beginning each item with an action verb.
- Review the final presentation – there should be a logical flow and a pleasing balance of concise text, images and white space.
- Practice the timing of the presentation and navigating forward and backward with the slides.
- Focus on the content; be confident, and make eye contact with the audience, not the PowerPoint.
- Allow time at the end for questions.

    – *Format*

- Develop the first slide to contain presentation title, presenter's name, e-mail address, organization, date.
- Number slides – choose Insert/Slide Number from the top menu; select 'Slide number' and 'Don't show on title slide'.
- Edit slides to an appropriate number; about one slide per minute is recommended.
- Cite sources and include an abbreviated Bibliography or Sources Cited slide if applicable.
- Conclude with a last slide that states something like 'Thank you for your attention. Any questions?'

Additional sources

Centre for Computing History:
   http://www.computinghistory.org.uk/
Computer History Museum:
   http://www.computerhistory.org/

'People and Computers,' by David Bohl:

http://ocean.otr.usm.edu/~w146169/people.html

'Six Degrees of J.C.R. Licklider Traces Computer Revolution,' by Dale Singer, *St Louis Post Dispatch*; originally published in *Everyday Magazine*, 29 August 2001, at:

http://dcl.wustl.edu/~jzacks/Psych4191/licklider_stlpd/lick.html

'Timeline of Events in Computer History':

http://www.computerhistory.org/timeline/

Notes

1. *The Free On-line Dictionary of Computing*, at: *http://foldoc.org/* (accessed 6 July 2008).
2. John Walker, 'The Analytical Engine: the first computer,' at: *http://www.fourmilab.ch/babbage/* (accessed 6 July 2008).
3. Frank da Cruz, 'Herman Hollerith Tabulating Machine,' Columbia University Computing History, at: *http://www.columbia.edu/acis/history/hollerith.html* (accessed 9 September 2009).
4. Andrew Hodges, 'Alan Turing Home Page,' at: *http://www.turing.org.uk/turing/* (accessed 9 September 2009).
5. Arthur Oldehoeft, Iowa State University, 'John Vincent Atanasoff and the birth of the digital computer,' at: *http://www.cs.iastate.edu/jva/jva-archive.shtml* (accessed 9 September 2009).
6. Kevin W. Richey, Virginia Tech University, 'The ENIAC,' at: *http://ei.cs.vt.edu/~history/ENIAC.Richey.HTML* (accessed 9 September 2009).
7. Smithsonian Natural Museum of American History, 'Computer History Collection,' at: *http://americanhistory.si.edu/collections/comphist/objects/univac.htm* (accessed 9 September 2009).
8. Lawrence Livermore National Laboratory, 'From kilobytes to petabytes in 50 years,' at: *https://www.llnl.gov/str/March02/pdfs/03_02.4.pdf* (accessed 9 September 2009).
9. IBM Archives, '1401 Data Processing System,' *http://www-03.ibm.com/ibm/history/exhibits/mainframe/mainframe_PP1401.html* (accessed 9 September 2009).
10. Texas Instruments, 'History of Innovation,' at: *http://www.ti.com/corp/docs/company/history/interactivetimeline.shtml* (accessed 9 September 2009).
11. OSData.com, 'History of operating systems,' at: *http://www.osdata.com/kind/history.htm* (accessed 9 September 2009).
12. John Markoff, *New York Times*, 23 May 2009, 'The future of artificial intelligence: the coming superbrain,' at: *http://www.nytimes.com/2009/05/24/weekinreview/24markoff.html* (accessed 9 September 2009).
13. Word processing exercise developed by Sharon Davis, 2007.

8

Network literacy: the Internet and the World Wide Web

The Internet is becoming the town square for the global village of tomorrow. (Bill Gates)

When and why was the first computer network developed?

ARPAnet

Just as the Second World War accelerated the development of modern computers, the Cold War fueled the development of the Internet. Although scientists who worked on the network claim that their purpose was to share computer resources, the US Department of Defense funded it as a research project to enhance national defense.

The post-Second World War Cold War climate in the US was marked by fear of Russian communist expansion and aggression after Russia tested its first atomic bomb in 1949. This fear was intensified when Russia launched the first space satellite, Sputnik, in 1957.[1]

According to their website (*http://www.arpa.mil*), the US Defense Advanced Research Projects Agency (DARPA) was

> created as the Advanced Research Projects Agency (ARPA) in February 1958. Its creation was directly attributed to the launching of Sputnik and to U.S. realization that the Soviet Union had developed the capacity to rapidly exploit military technology. Additionally, the political and defense communities recognized the need for a high-level DoD (Department of Defense) organization to

formulate and execute R&D (research and development) projects that would expand the frontiers of technology beyond the immediate and specific requirements of the Military Services and their laboratories.[2]

ARPAnet → NSFnet → Internet

NSFnet

ARPAnet evolved into NSFnet, which later evolved into the Internet. Along the way, the Internet passed from government control to private enterprise and commercialization. While law enforcement agencies sometimes monitor the Internet for illegal activity, no one person or organization owns it.

The National Science Foundation (NSF) was founded by Congress and President Truman in 1950 to 'promote the progress of science; to advance the national health, prosperity, and welfare; to secure the national defense; and for other purposes.'[3]

By the late 1970s, ARPAnet was beginning to have a tremendous impact so the NSF began developing a high-speed network to replace ARPAnet. This main network, also known as the *backbone*, grew to connect smaller regional, national, and international networks. 'Between 1990 and late 1994 the pieces of NSFnet were sold to major telecommunications companies until the Internet backbone had gone completely commercial.'[4]

Internet

While ARPAnet was just one network, it quickly evolved into a 'network of networks.' According to Vint Cerf, 'This was called the Inter-netting project and the system of networks which emerged from the research was known as the "Internet."'[5]

The Internet may be thought of not only geographically[6] but also metaphorically.

In *Poetics*, Book XXII, Aristotle said 'a poet must have a command of metaphor. This alone cannot be imparted by another; it is the mark of genius, for to make good metaphors implies an eye for resemblances.'[7]

Chou (1998) stated in the *Internet Activities Newsletter* that the Internet is not just the information superhighway (earth) or surfing the Web (water), but about air (instant communication) and fire (illumination of mind and spirit). The Internet is a mind-place for spiritual communion and celebration. Lao Tzu says 'The net of heaven is cast wide' (Tao Te Ching, LXXIII) and the word 'inter' may be interpreted as 'between terra' so that Internet is 'between earth and heaven'.[8]

Internet2

Since the commercialization of the Internet, there has been an effort to develop a new not-for-profit network that returns to the original purpose of the Internet: education and research. Internet2, as detailed on its website, was developed by the research and education community in 1996 and

> promotes the missions of its members by providing both leading-edge network capabilities and unique partnership opportunities ... By bringing research and academia together with technology leaders from industry, government and the international community, Internet2 promotes collaboration and innovation that has a fundamental impact on the future of the Internet.[9]

Computer network timeline

(Adapted from Hobbes' Internet Timeline)[10]

1945–50s

- The US was the only nuclear power until 1949 when Russia tested their first atomic bomb.
- In 1952, the US developed the hydrogen bomb and by 1953 Russia also had the H-bomb.
- The 1950s was the era of bomb shelters and bomb drills in schools (duck and cover).

1957

- Russia put Sputnik, the first man-made satellite, into space and the West feared Russian dominance in science and technology.

- Kruschev said to the US 'We will bury you' and the US feared the 'red threat' of communist domination, so during the Cold War there was increased government funding for scientific research and development.

1964

- Packet-switching technology (groups of data bits relayed through a computer network) was funded by the US Department of Defense which wanted a communication network system with no central headquarters that could be destroyed in a nuclear attack.

1969

- ARPAnet created by the Pentagon's Advanced Research Projects Agency with computer sites (nodes) at four research universities so scientists could share files.

1972

- Thirty-seven sites or nodes in ARPAnet (universities, US government research facilities).
- Network protocols developed to allow computers to transfer data. TCP/IP (Transmission Control Protocol/Internet Protocol) converts messages into packets of 1,500 bytes and reassembles them at the receiving end.
- First public demo of e-mail that allowed users to communicate.

Early Net applications

Studies have shown that the number one use of the Internet is for communication. Until the 1990s, communication as well as other computer network applications were *text-based*.

Electronic mail (e-mail) based on the protocol 'user log-in name @ host computer name' was first developed in 1971 by Ray Tomlinson of ARPAnet.[11]

Two other early network applications, *Telnet* and *FTP*, allowed more efficient communication and file-sharing. Telnet allows a strong, direct connection from a computer to a distant server. FTP (file transfer protocol) is a means to transfer files, particularly large files, in an efficient manner.[12]

Vinton Cerf, 'Father of the Internet'

Vint Cerf played a major role in the development of protocols, or telecommunications standards, of Internet packet-switching technology. In 1976, Cerf was a DARPA program manager in charge of packet technology and inter-netting research. The TCP/IP, or Transmission Control Protocol/Internet Protocol, developed by his team at ARPA, checks data packets for errors and reassembles the packets in the correct sequential order at the destination site. These packet-switching standard protocols allow consistent and universal data transmissions.[13]

Joseph Carl Robnett (Lick) Licklider, 'Visionary from Missouri'

Licklider, a professor of psychology of communications, worked at DARPA's Information Processing Techniques Office. In 1960, Licklider wrote:

> It seems reasonable to envision, for a time 10 or 15 years hence, a 'thinking center' that will incorporate the functions of present-day libraries together with anticipated advances in information storage and retrieval. The picture readily enlarges itself into a network of such centers, connected to one another by wide-band communication lines and to individual users by leased-wire services. In such a system, the speed of the computers would be balanced, and the cost of the gigantic memories and the sophisticated programs would be divided by the number of users.[14]

In *Libraries of the Future* (1965), Licklider wrote about how a computer could provide an automated library with simultaneous remote use by many different people through access to a common database.[15]

Computer connectivity: client-server

Computers are connected together in networks that are organized as clients and servers.

- *Clients* are personal computers or computer workstations.

- *Servers* are large central computers that hold large collections of data and programs. Data from personal computers are routed through larger servers to connect to other networks.

- *ISPs*, or Internet service providers, provide connectivity through a larger server, such as AOL or Comcast cable.

Domain name system (DNS)[16]

Just as every telephone has a unique number, every computer connected to the Internet has a unique address or *URL* (uniform resource locator) that includes the individual or organization name plus a domain name, such as: *http://www.usm.edu*.

Originally, there were six primary top level domain names and these are still the most common:

- .COM for commercial
- .NET for network
- .ORG for organization
- .EDU for education
- .MIL for military
- .GOV for government.

Recently, seven new top-level domains (TLDs) have been approved by ICANN (Internet Corporation for Assigned Names and Numbers: *http://www.icann.org/*), the global, non-profit organization that coordinates the DNS:

- .AERO for air-transport industry
- .BIZ for businesses
- .COOP for cooperatives
- .INFO for all uses
- .MUSEUM for museums
- .NAME for individuals
- .PRO for professions.

If an Internet address does not contain a country code in the domain name (for example, the British Library URL, *http://www.bl.uk/*), then it is most likely a US-based Internet site. A two-letter *country code* is generally used to identify other non-US countries of origin.[17]

What is the World Wide Web?

Tim Berners-Lee developed the World Wide Web in late 1990 while working at CERN, the European Particle Physics Laboratory in Geneva, Switzerland. What the Web added to the Internet was the ability to display graphics and multimedia as well as hypertext (interactive links).

Berners-Lee traces the beginnings for the idea of the Web in his 1999 book, *Weaving the Web: The Original Design and Ultimate Destiny of the World Wide Web*:

> I am the son of mathematicians ... One day when I came home from high school, I found my father working on a speech ... He was reading books on the brain, looking for clues about how to make a computer intuitive, able to complete connections as the brain did. We discussed the point; then my father went on to his speech and I went on to my homework. But the idea stayed with me that computers could become much more powerful if they could be programmed to link otherwise unconnected information ... Suppose all the information stored on computers everywhere were linked, I thought. Suppose I could program my computer to create a space in which anything could be linked to anything ... There would be a single, global information space.[18]

Berners-Lee cites these men and their ideas or inventions as the building blocks for the Web:

- Vannevar Bush wrote 'As We May Think' in 1945 about the concept of a machine he called Mimex, which used binary coding, photocells and instant photography to cross-reference microfilm.[19]

- Doug Engelbart, a researcher at Stanford, invented what he called a *mouse*, first demonstrated in 1968, to steer his computer's cursor across the screen.[20]

- In 1981, Ted Nelson wrote *Literary Machines* that described Xanadu, a non-linear hypertext format with embedded links in all its documents.[21]

- Berners-Lee and his colleagues at CERN developed the computer language of the Web, known as *Hypertext Markup Language* (*HTML*), but they had a problem ... how to display the graphics and hypertext on a computer screen that was text-only. In response to this problem, they developed a program known as a *browser* to access the Web. Soon, more complex browsers were developed to take advantage of the Web's hypertext and graphics capabilities.

- Michael Grobe and other students at the University of Kansas developed a text-only hypertext browser, *Lynx* (*lynx.isc.org/*), in around 1992.

- In 1993 an early successful hypertext and graphics-capable browser, *Mosaic* (*mosaic.org/*), was developed at the National Center for Supercomputing Applications (NCSA) at the University of Illinois by graduate students who made it freely available over the Web.

- The first successful commercially available browser (1994) was *Netscape* (*netscape.com*) produced by Mosaic Communications Corporation.

- In 1995, Bill Gates' company, Microsoft, released *Internet Explorer* (*http://www.microsoft.com/windows/internet-explorer/*).

- In 2004, Mozilla released the open-source (free) browser *Firefox* (*http://www.mozilla.com/firefox/*).[22]

What is Web 2.0?

Web 2.0, coined by O'Reilly Media in 2004, refers to a second generation of web-based applications (such as social networking sites, blogs and wikis) that facilitate collaboration and sharing between users.[23]

Web 2.0 is based on a new version of Hypertext Markup Language known as *Extensible Markup Language* (*XML*) that extends HTML's capabilities.

- Web-logs or *blogs* are web pages that provide publication of web links or comments on a specific topic, often in the form of short entries arranged in reverse chronological order. Some blogs accept postings from its readers.[24]

- *Wikis*, based on a Hawaiian term meaning 'quick' or 'informal,' are a web application that allows users to add content to a collaborative web resource (co-authoring) and permits others to edit that content (open editing).[25]

- *User-generated content* or *UGC* allows users to create web content (more on this in the next chapter).

What will the Web be in the future? Web 3.0: the semantic web

The World Wide Web Consortium (W3C) defined the *semantic web* as one that 'provides a common framework that allows data to be shared and reused across application, enterprise, and community boundaries ... It is based on the Resource Description Framework (RDF).'[26] RDF requires each web page to have more descriptive information tags in the code so that it can be more easily linked to pages with similar content.

The developers of the World Wide Web, Berners-Lee et al., described the semantic web (Web 3.0) in a 2001 article in *Scientific American* as a more intelligent and useful Web in which software agents roaming across the Web can carry out tasks, infer when information is needed, and provide that information. According to the authors:

> Knowledge representation, as this technology is often called, is currently in a state comparable to that of hypertext before the advent of the Web: it is clearly a good idea, and some very nice demonstrations exist, but it has not yet changed the world.[27]

Web directories and search engines

Web directories and search engines are very different but are typically paired together. For instance, Yahoo.com is primarily a directory, but has added a robotic search engine to search the directory. For a more detailed comparison of indexes/directories with search engines see CyberMetrics (*http://www.cindoc.csic.es/cybermetrics/search01.html*).

Web indexes or directories

Web indexes or directories are lists of *human-selected* web resources organized by topic. A comparison of web subject directories by Greg Notess is available at: *http://searchengineshowdown.com/dir/*.

The quality of websites found in directories depends on the human indexers. The best web directories are indexed by subject specialists who are experts in their field. One example of an expert-compiled directory is *The Scout Report* (*http://scout.cs.wisc.edu/*), sponsored by the University of Wisconsin-Madison, who used their access to highly educated content specialists to create and update an annotated directory of recommended web resources.

Web search engines

Web search engines are databases generated by *robotic (non-human) programs* known as spiders, bots, wanderers, web walkers, or agents.

Search engine features include:

- full-text indexing of website contents;
- advanced, complex search strategy support, such as Boolean searching capability.

To become more knowledgeable about the newest search engines and search engine features, explore *Search Engine Watch (http://searchenginewatch.com/)*.

Google revolution

One of the most popular and innovative search engines is *Google.com*. Before Google, it was becoming increasingly difficult to find appropriate and relevant websites since commercial website developers would add misleading descriptors to their web code that would cause the search engines to retrieve their website while looking for something else. Google changed that by using a mathematical formula or 'weighting algorithm' to compute relevance. The secret, proprietary formula ranks a website not only by popularity, but by relevance of the sites that it links to and that link to it. For instance, having a large number of .edu or .gov websites that link to a particular website will boost the ranking of that site. Google Guide (*http://www.googleguide.com/google_works.html*) has more information about how Google works.

In addition to statistical ranking, Google.com has introduced many innovative features that are now copied by other search engines. Each search engine is slightly different, however, and research indicates that there is only about a 40 per cent overlap in the search results of the various search engines.

Bing

Bing.com is a new Microsoft search engine. Bing finds and organizes the information so the user can make faster, more informed decisions. Bing also has interactive maps and satellite images similar to Google Earth (*http://earth.Google.com*).

Meta versus specialized searching

There are two opposing directional trends in web searching:

- meta-searching;
- specialized searching.

Meta-searching searches multiple search engines at once, such as www.37.com that searches 37 search engines at one time, Dogpile.com, or Mamma.com.

Specialized search engines search on a specialized topic. Some examples include:

- *FindLaw.com* for legal information;
- *SearchEdu.com* for educational information.

Internet archive

One common complaint about Internet resources is the occurrence of broken links or disappearing websites. Attempts have been made to alleviate this problem by archiving websites:

- Google.com archives the text of its websites. Search for a term in Google and notice that one option is a link to a 'cached' site of the archived text. One drawback is that the graphics are usually not archived.
- The Internet Archive (*http://www.archive.org*) has a 'Wayback Machine' that one can search for archived websites. This is useful to find electronic documents or websites that no longer exist or, since the websites are archived by date, to examine how a particular website changes over time.

Exercises

Exercise 1

1. Visit a web glossary such as *Net Lingo* (*http://www.netlingo.com/dictionary/all.php*) and translate the terms and acronyms below into English.

LOL	PAL	PML
ROTFL	PAW	OTOH
ROTFLMAO	BTW	AFAIK
IMHO	FYI	ASAP
JMHO	H&G	FWIW

Exercise 2

Keep an 'Internet usage' journal for one week. Include one entry for each day. Include the following information in each entry:

1. How long you spent on the Internet each day (total hours).

2. What types of things you did on the Internet – e-mail, Internet searching for school, Internet searching for entertainment, Web 2.0 activities such as Facebook, MySpace, YouTube, gaming, conducting business, or other. List these activities and approximately how much time you spent on each.

3. At the end of the week, look at your journal entries. Compile a list of the top five activities you engaged in on the Internet. List how much time you spent for the total week on the Internet. Do you feel that the time you spent on the Internet is typical for you in a given week? Do you feel that the activities you engaged in are typical for you in a given week? Why, or why not? Do you think that your Internet usage will increase or decrease in the future? Why do you think it will increase or decrease?

Exercise 3

1. List 4–5 changes that you believe we will see in the Internet over the next 10–15 years.

2. In addition, list 3–5 changes that you would like to see.

Exercise 4

Search in three different search engines (e.g. Scout Report, Google, and Bing) a topic of your choice such as 'information literacy.'

1. List the top five results retrieved with each search engine.

2. Did any of the retrieved websites appear in two of the lists? If so, how many?

3. Did any of the retrieved websites appear in all three of the lists? If so, how many?

Additional sources

'A Little History of the World Wide Web':
  http://www.w3.org/History.html
'An Atlas of Cyberspace':
  *http://personalpages.manchester.ac.uk/staff/m.dodge/cybergeography//
  atlas/historical.html*
Best of the Web directory:
  http://botw.org/
'Evaluating Web Content,' by SUNY Albany Library:
  http://library.albany.edu/usered/eval/evalweb/
'Internet Growth Chart,' by Russ Haynal:
  http://navigators.com/stats.html
Internet Pioneer – Tim Berners-Lee:
  http://www.ibiblio.org/pioneers/lee.html
Interview with Jakob Nielsen, podcast by IT Conversations:
  http://itc.conversationsnetwork.org/shows/detail670.html
'Realising the full potential of the Web,' by Tim Berners-Lee, 1997:
  http://www.w3.org/1998/02/Potential.html
Search Engine Colossus: 'Search Engines from Around the World':
  http://www.searchenginecolossus.com/
'Web Power Searching Tips,' from Search Engine Watch:
  http://searchenginewatch.com/2156031

Notes

1. Eleanor Roosevelt National Historic Site, 'The Eleanor Roosevelt Papers: Cold War,' at: *http://www.nps.gov/archive/elro/glossary/cold-war.htm* (accessed 10 September 2009).
2. Defense Advance Research Projects Agency (DARPA), 'DARPA History,' at: *http://www.arpa.mil/history.html* (accessed 10 September 2009).
3. National Science Foundation (NSF), 'NSF at a Glance,' at: *http://www.nsf.gov/about/glance.jsp* (accessed 9 September 2009).
4. DieNet Dictionary, 'Internet,' at: *http://dictionary.die.net/internet* (accessed 12 September 2009).

5. Internet Society (ISOC), 'A Brief History of the Internet,' at: *http:// www.isoc.org/internet/history/brief.shtml* (accessed 12 September 2009).

6. Martin Dodge, 'An Atlas of Cyberspace,' at: *http://personalpages.manchester .ac.uk/staff/m.dodge/cybergeography//atlas/geographic.html* (accessed 9 September 2009).

7. The Internet Classics Archive, 'Poetics' by Aristotle, translated by S.H. Butcher, at: *http://classics.mit.edu/Aristotle/poetics.3.3.html* (accessed 9 September 2009).

8. Peter Y. Chou (1998) *Internet Activities Newsletter*, Issue 1, at: *http://www .wisdomportal.com/Internet/Issue-June29.html* (accessed 9 September 2009).

9. Internet2, at: *http://www.internet2.edu/* (accessed 25 September 2009).

10. Robert Hobbes Zakon, 'Hobbes' Internet Timeline,' at: *http://www.zakon .org/robert/internet/timeline/* (accessed 10 September 2009).

11. Richard T. Griffiths, 'History of Electronic Mail,' at: *http://www.let .leidenuniv.nl/history/ivh/chap3.htm* (accessed 9 September 2009).

12. Judy Still, 'Introduction to Telnet, FTP, and Gopher,' at: *http://www.rci .rutgers.edu/~au/workshop/telnet.htm* (accessed 9 September 2009).

13. Internet Corporation for Assigned Names and Numbers (ICANN), 'Vinton G. Cerf, Vice President and Chief Internet Evangelist, Google,' at: *http:// www.icann.org/en/biog/cerf.htm* (accessed 9 September 2009).

14. J.C.R. Licklider, 'Man–Computer Symbiosis,' at: *http://memex.org/licklider .pdf* (accessed 9 September 2009).

15. David S. Bennahum, 'J.C.R. Licklider (1915–1990),' at: *http://memex.org/ licklider.html* (accessed 9 September 2009).

16. InterNIC, 'The Domain Name System: A Non-Technical Explanation – Why Universal Resolvability Is Important,' at: *http://www.internic.net/faqs/ authoritative-dns.html* (accessed 7 September 2009).

17. Internet Assigned Numbers Authority (IANA), 'Root Zone Database,' at: *http://www.iana.org/domains/root/db/* (accessed 8 September 2009).

18. Tim Berners-Lee (1999) *Weaving the Web: The Original Design and Ultimate Destiny of the World Wide Web*. New York: HarperOne.

19. Vannevar Bush (1945) 'As We May Think,' *Atlantic Monthly*, July, at: *http:// www.ps.uni-sb.de/~duchier/pub/vbush/vbush.shtml* (accessed 2 July 2009).

20. Doug Engelbart Institute, 'A Lifetime Pursuit,' at: *http://www.dougengelbart .org/history/engelbart.html* (accessed 2 July 2009).

21. Ted Nelson (1981) *Literary Machines*. Sausalito, CA: Mindful Press.

22. Brian Wilson, 'Browser Timeline,' at: *http://www.blooberry.com/indexdot/ history/browsers.htm* (accessed 2 July 2009).

23. Tim O'Reilly, 'What Is Web 2.0: Design Patterns and Business Models for the Next Generation of Software,' at: *http://www.oreillynet.com/pub/a/ oreilly/tim/news/2005/09/30/what-is-web-20.html* (accessed 7 July 2009).

24. Joan M. Reitz, *ODLIS – Online Dictionary for Library and Information Science*, at: *http://lu.com/odlis/odlis_w.cfm#weblog* (accessed 7 July 2009).

25. Joan M. Reitz, *ODLIS – Online Dictionary for Library and Information Science*, at: *http://lu.com/odlis/odlis_W.cfm#wiki* (accessed 7 July 2009).

26. World Wide Web Consortium, 'W3C Semantic Web Activity,' at: *http://www.w3.org/2001/sw/* (accessed 21 June 2009).

27. Tim Berners-Lee, James Hindler, and Ora Lassila (2001) 'The Semantic Web', *Scientific American*, 284(5): 34–44.

9

Media literacy and visual literacy

Today we are beginning to notice that the new media are not just mechanical gimmicks for creating worlds of illusion, but new languages with new and unique powers of expression. (Marshall McLuhan)

What is media literacy?

'Media' (and its singular form 'medium') is from the Latin *medius*, meaning 'middle' or 'between two things.' The Canadian Marshall McLuhan (1911–80) was the first to use this term to mean 'means of mass communication.'

Media literacy is defined by the Trent Think Tank on Media Literacy as 'the ability to decode, analyze, evaluate, and produce communication in a variety of forms.'[1] According to the Information Competence Project at California Polytechnic State University, a person who is media literate:

- has the ability to assess the credibility of information received as well as the credibility of the information source;
- has the ability to recognize metaphor and uses of symbols in entertainment, advertising, and political commentary;
- has the ability to discern between appeals to emotion and logic, and recognizes covert and overt appeals;
- is sensitive to verbal as well as visual arguments;
- has the ability to use critical faculties to assess the truth of information gleaned from various sources.[2]

The empowerment approach was advocated by Johnson, in 'Digital Literacy: Re-Thinking Education and Training in a Digital World':

- Media literacy is essential for citizenship.
- The media are powerful social and cultural forces.
- The media are social constructions.
- Audiences are active creators of their own meaning.[3]

The Ancient Greeks believed it was vital for a democratic society and government to have literate and educated citizens. According to the empowerment approach, it is equally important in the digital information age to be media literate – to be able to *understand*, *evaluate*, and *use* digital, multimedia information. As McLuhan noted, the new media are *new languages* and one must be fluent in those languages to be considered media literate.

What are 'old media' and 'new media'?

Old media

The old, traditional media, also known as mainstream media (MSM), are controlled by large news organizations and publishers:

- print newspapers and magazines;
- television or radio broadcasting – broadcasting was originally an agricultural term, referring to the casting of seeds over a large area. Later it came to mean the communication of information across a wide area (the opposite of broadcasting is narrowcasting, or communicating information to a very narrow, targeted audience).

New media

The new media, based on Web 2.0 technology, include user-generated content (UGC), push technologies, and e-media.
User-generated content (UGC) allows users to create and edit content:

- *web pages* using code such as HTML or XML;
- web logs or *blogs* such as Instapundit (*pajamasmedia.com/instapundit/*);
- *wikis*, such as Wikipedia (*Wikipedia.org*);
- *social-networking* sites, such as Facebook (*Facebook.com*);
- *social brief-communication* sites such as Twitter (*twitter.com*);

- *photo-sharing* sites, such as Flickr (*Flickr.com*);
- *video-sharing* sites, such as YouTube (*YouTube.com*).

Push technologies are e-content sent from the server to the client:

- *podcasting* (audio or video files such as those at *PodcastAlley.com*) or *webcasting* (live audio or video over the Web such as *Webcastingzone.com*);
- *RSS*, which stands for either 'really simple syndication' or 'rich site summary' (see *http://www.whatisrss.com/*), is a subscription news-feed service that delivers news items or updates to a computer. One good example is the BBC RSS (*http://news.bbc.co.uk/2/hi/help/3223484.stm*);
- *intelligent agents* are programs that assist users in performing specific computer-related tasks (*www.agentland.com/*).

E-media

Old media are increasingly becoming digital and multimedia. Some media exist both in print and online and some exist only in e-format. News about e-media can be found at *http://www.poynter.org/*.

Digital media

- Online newspapers (*http://www.onlinenewspapers.com*)
- Internet radio directory (*http://radiotower.com*)
- Digital television and movie episodes (*http://www.hulu.com*)

Desktop digital reference sources

- NY Times Reference for Journalists (*http://www.nytimes.com/library/cyber/reference/*)
- RefDesk.com, Online Reference Desk

Digital fun and games

- Library Science Jeopardy (*http://terpconnect.umd.edu/~aubrycp/project/jeopardy.html*)

- Web Puzzler (*http://www.briancasey.org/artifacts/puzzle/*)
- Games.com

New media pioneers and rebels

- Ted Turner founded the first all-news cable network, CNN, in Atlanta in1980.[4]
- Robert L. Johnson founded Black Entertainment Television in 1980; BET became the first African-American-controlled company to be traded publicly on the NY Stock Exchange.[5]
- Rupert Murdoch is the controversial Australian media mogul who owns the News Corporation Company, a worldwide media enterprise.[6]
- Matt Drudge, with no college education or journalism background, founded the e-news website, DrudgeReport.com, in the 1990s.[7]

What is computer-mediated communication?

What is meant by the medium is the message?

McLuhan maintained that the new electronic media not only greatly affect or change the message, they also change the way humans process information and therefore change society. Thus he was fond of saying that the medium is the message. According to McLuhan, each new medium extends some senses and amputates others. In a 1998 article, Katz and Katz state that McLuhan

> tells us to pay less attention to the content of a medium than to its technology. The message, he implies, is what the medium tells us about *how* to think, not what to think ... (the medium is the message). The electronic age has extended several of our senses simultaneously, and, through the awareness of ourselves and others that is said to be the product of such multidimensional involvement, we are better able to understand, and assume responsibility for, what is happening in our community, our nation, and our planet ... hence the concept of 'global village.' McLuhan

contrasts the selfishness of typographic culture with the collectivism of electronic culture.[8]

Computer-mediated communication (CMC) is digital communication between two or more people via a computer. It may include any interactive digital communication such as e-mail, listservs (electronic discussion groups), instant messaging, blogs, wikis, social networks, or virtual online environments.

Some CMC, such as listservs or wikis, may be moderated and the content controlled. One must be aware that most digital communication is archived and easily forwarded, copied, or stored so CMC must be considered to be in the public domain.

Never use CMC for personal, confidential, sensitive, or defamatory information – electronic, digital communication such as e-mail and text-messaging is not secure. Instead, use it wisely and effectively by following the rules of netiquette.

CMC netiquette

Netiquette refers to the rules of etiquette in digital communications.

- Do not type in all capital letters unless the message is urgent or important. (Words all in capital letters are equivalent to shouting.)
- Do not *spam*, or send annoying e-mails; do not send chain e-mails or very large files via e-mail.
- Do not *flame*, or send insulting or offensive messages (a flamer sends offensive messages; a firefighter or peacemaker puts out flames).
- Be careful in opening attachments – viruses are spread through attachments so install a virus-protection program.
- Do not send unsolicited, large files via e-mail.
- Do not send anything defamatory, gossipy, or negative about someone in an e-mail; remember, it can easily be forwarded to that person.
- Do not put personal, confidential, sensitive, or defamatory information in an e-mail – *e-mail and other forms of CMC are not secure.*
- Do not use e-mail inappropriately using workplace computers – employers frequently monitor employees' e-mail with specialized software.

Do use e-mail and other forms of CMC wisely:

- Strive for a personable, professional and businesslike tone.
- Always type in a brief, descriptive, and appropriate title in the subject line.
- Create a signature file so that each e-mail that you send has basic information as a signature such as name and organization.
- Organize e-mail into folders; keep your inbox empty by moving e-mail into relevant folders and deleting junk e-mail.

For more detailed tips on writing effective e-mails for personal and business communication, see 'Writing Effective E-Mail: Top 10 Tips' (*http://jerz.setonhill.edu/writing/e-text/e-mail.htm*) by Jessica Bauer and Dennis G. Jerz.

What is visual literacy?

Visual literacy as defined by the International Visual Literacy Association is 'a group of vision competencies a human being can develop by seeing and at the same time having and integrating other sensory experiences.'[9]

John Debes (1969) defines visual literacy as a set of competencies that 'enable a visually literate person to discriminate and interpret the visual actions, objects, and/or symbols, natural or man-made, that are encountered in the environment. Through the creative use of these competencies, we are able to communicate with others.'[10]

Visualization of information

Visualization of information is different from but related to information literacy. Visualization of information focuses on displaying data visually to enhance understanding and perhaps to detect patterns.

The leader and guru in the field of information visualization, Edward Tufte, a Professor Emeritus at Yale University, has written books and taught courses on information design.[11]

Tufte's Meta-Principle of Visual Information Design is 'to make good thinking visible equals good information design ... Good design is clear thinking made visible.'[12]

Tufte's Principles of Visual Information Design

1. *Enforce visual comparisons: compared with what?*[13] Put images to be compared side-by-side, which makes it easier for the reader to see the similarities and differences in the images.

2. *Show cause and effects: why the change?*[14] Make concepts and ideas as clear as possible. If you are creating a visual showing the causes of erosion in land, make the connection between the causes of erosion and the effects on the land very clear.

3. *Display multivariate information: in relationship to what?*[15] Use multiple images to illustrate a concept, idea, or theme.

4. *Abstracted information needs some narrative to address to what end?*[16] Visuals also need text which further explains their content.

5. *Integrate text, numbers, images into a complete picture based on quality, relevance and integrity of content.*[17] Use text, numbers, and images together to create a total 'package' of information.

Examples of good design and bad design

According to Tufte, the one of the best examples of the visual display of data is Charles Joseph Minard's 1861 graphic showing Napoleon's losses during his 1812 march to and from Moscow. The visual displays the route of the army to and from Moscow, the size of the army, the temperature during the march and the time frame.[18]

An example of bad design is related to the Space Shuttle Challenger accident in 1986, in which seven astronauts were killed when the shuttle exploded. The temperature was cold that morning and the engineers tried to convince NASA to delay the flight. Tufte maintains that the chart used by Morton-Thiokol, the maker of the space shuttle's solid-fuel rocket boosters, to present their case was not effective and a simple, clearer relational chart would have made the case for delay stronger (see a comparison of the two charts at the bottom of *http://www.evl.uic .edu/aej/422/week02.html*).

Spatial analysis

Spatial analysis seeks to find patterns in the visual display of information. Spatial analysis is usually done geographically and has many applications including crime-mapping and determining disease patterns.

One of the earliest documented examples of spatial analysis is the example of Dr John Snow. Snow was a British doctor who in the course of trying to determine the source of cholera, located every cholera death in the Soho district of London and marked the location of each victim on a map. Dr Snow noticed that the pattern of dots clustered around the Broad Street water pump. He closed that pump and the epidemic was stopped.[19]

Modern spatial analysis may be conducted through GIS, geographic information systems, software that can query and display data geographically in order to analyze patterns. The largest GIS company is ESRI (*esri.com*), which produces the ArcView desktop GIS.

- An example of an online interactive GIS system is: *http://www .MapQuest.com*.

- US Census data maps may be found at: *http://factfinder.census.gov*.

- Try the free download version of Google Earth at: *http://earth.google .com/*.

Digital multimedia collections

Increasingly, libraries are digitizing primary-source, archival materials so they are accessible to people via the Web. Some examples are:

- Abraham Lincoln Historical Digitization Project: *http://lincoln.lib.niu .edu/*

- Library of Congress American Memory at: *http://memory.loc.gov*

- Cornell Library Windows on the Past: *http://cdl.library.cornell.edu/*

- University of Missouri Marr Sound Archives: *http://library.umkc.edu/ marr-digitalprojects*

- University of Missouri Kansas City Book of Gregorian Chant: *http:// library.umkc.edu/spec-col/chantbook/main.htm*

Free online books

- Online Books Page, a list of over 20,000 online books by the University of Pennsylvania: *http://digital.library.upenn.edu/books/*

- International Children's Digital Library, free children's books online by the University of Maryland: *http://en.childrenslibrary.org/*

- Free Audio Books: *http://www.simplyaudiobooks.com/Free_Audiobooks/ dp/202/*
- New York Public Library's Digital Public Library: *http://www.nypl .org/digital/*

Exercises

Exercise 1

The medium is the message:

1. Watch the video on YouTube at: *http://www.youtube.com/watch?v= FSIkjNaICsg*.
2. What is the message? Why do you think this medium was used? What is the creator of the video saying about our society?

Exercise 2

1. Assume that you are teaching someone who has never been on the Internet the 'rules' for surfing the Web. Create a list of 10–12 'rules' or guidelines that someone new to the Internet would need to know before they began using the web. For example, 'Don't type in ALL CAPITAL LETTERS because people will think you are angry with them' would be an appropriate guideline.

Exercise 3

Computer-mediated communication:

1. Create a signature file for your e-mail account. From the Inbox page, look for an 'Options' button, then look for either 'Edit Personal Information' or 'Signature' option. Create or edit your default identity or signature file, depending on the e-mail. Type in and save the information you would like to have as an auto signature for each e-mail sent (in some e-mail programs, you must click on 'Change' to save). Send a test e-mail with your signature file to the instructor.
2. Organize your e-mail account: create or edit folders with logical categories to store all of the e-mail that should be saved. For

instance, a student should create a folder for each course. How many folders were created? List folder titles.

3. Use L-Soft (*http://www.lsoft.com/lists/list_q.html*) or one of the lists at Yale University's 'Scholarly Communication: Finding and Joining a List' (*http://www.library.yale.edu/ref/internet-comm/list.html*) to search for and subscribe to a listserv (group discussion list) in an academic/professional area of your choice (a great resource for jobs/internships, etc.). What is the name of the listserv? Forward the welcoming e-mail to the instructor.

Exercise 4

Open a Google account and create a scholarly blog at blogger.com.

A blog is an online journal and this one should be a record of academic or cultural activities, such as museum or gallery exhibits or other scholarly or cultural activities.

Each blog should have at least three postings or entries and each posting should contain at least *three* elements:

- descriptive or reflective text of at least one, but preferably two paragraphs;
- a related image;* and
- a link to the image or related website.

Blog instructions

1. If you do not have a g-mail account, open an account at: *http://mail.google.com/*.
2. Go to *http://www.blogger.com*.
3. Click on 'Create Your Blog Now.'
4. Click 'Continue' and sign in with your g-mail account and password.
5. Give your blog a title and a web address (URL).
6. Click 'Continue.'
7. Choose a template. (How do you want the background of the blog to look?)
8. Click 'Start Posting.'
9. Type in an appropriate title and text (or paste in text that is already created such as your cultural essay); add an appropriate web link with the posting.

10. To add a web link, highlight the text or URL that you want to be the link then click on the icon with the green globe and type or paste in an appropriate link. Click 'OK' then publish the post.

11. Click on the 'Add Image' icon on the menu; browse and locate an image file (or find an image on the Web); choose a layout then click on 'Upload Image.'

12. Click on 'View Blog' to see what your posting looks like; if you wish to edit, click on 'Customize' or 'Dashboard' to access the Settings option or Posting option to edit posts.

13. To add an RSS feed subscription, click on 'Settings' then 'Layout' option then 'Add a Gadget.' Locate the 'Feed' option and paste in an RSS subscription URL such as the one for the British Library: *http://feeds.feedburner.com/BritishLibraryPressReleases?format=xml*, or BBC News: *http://feeds.feedburner.com/bbcnewsfrontpagefullfeed.*

14. To edit posts or add a new post to your blog, go to your blog address and sign in then click on 'New Post' or 'Edit Post' and follow the directions above to add a new post with image and link.

Exercise 5

Learn basic HTML:

1. Complete the HTML tutorial at *http://www.w3schools.com/html.*
2. Take the HTML quiz.
3. Earn a certificate in HTML.

Exercise 6

Create a web page using the HTML code you learned in the HTML tutorial or follow the directions at: *http://ocean.otr.usm.edu/~w146169/ webpage.htm.*

There are free web editor software sites, but it is preferable to learn basic HTML or XML code so you can create a web page by typing in code or edit a web page created with software. Creating a web page from code is the most readable from any browser and the most accessible to disability-assisted software. It is also possible to create web pages and save as an html file using the free basic utility program 'Notepad' (in Windows: Start/Programs/Accessories/Notepad). The protocol to use for a web home page is to save it as 'index.html.'

HTML code is not copyrighted so you may be able to find web pages with simple code such as other students' web pages. You can then copy and revise that code with your own information (*http://ocean.otr.usm .edu/~w146169/StudentProjects.htm*).

- Click on a student's web page link.
- On the top menu, click on 'View' then 'Source.'
- A Notepad window with the web page code will pop up.
- Either 'Save as' ... 'index.html' and save to your desk top ... then edit.
- Or click on 'Edit' then 'Select All' then 'Copy' to a file in Arachnophilia (see the web page tutorial for the link) or other html editor, then edit.

The web page should contain the following elements:

- <blockquote> tag to create margins
- an image of your choice*
- web page title (your name)
- <hr> or horizontal rule
- podcast link (internal link – see instructions below)**
- bulleted list with at least three useful external links (links that include the entire URL)
- link to online résumé (internal link – see instructions below)***
- <hr> – another horizontal rule
- contact information (e-mail address) at the bottom
- 'Date Created' or 'Updated' date at the bottom
- if you have an account on your organization or institution's web server, upload the 'index.html' file and the other files that are internal links to the 'public_html' folder in your web account.

* How to find and save images from the Web

1. Go to Google.com.
2. Click on 'Images' at the top left corner to do an image search.
3. Search for 'public domain images,' click on an appropriate image, then click on 'See full size image.'
4. Place the cursor on the image then right click – a menu box will appear.
5. From the menu box, choose the option 'Save Image As ...'

6. Save the image to your desktop or to a disk.

7. Now the image is ready for you to upload onto the blog. Be sure to include the link to the image source (copy and paste the URL).

** How to create and add a podcast as an internal link

1. Download the free software Audacity (*audacity.sourceforge.net/*) to record and edit an audio greeting, or use a site that allows users to use a mobile phone to record an audio file such as AudioBoo (*audioboo.fm*) or Ipadio (*ipadio.com*).

2. Save your audio file as a wav file such as 'Homepage.wav' (or as an MP3 file).

3. Upload the audio file to your *ocean.otr.usm.edu* account public_html folder.

4. Add a link on your homepage (*index.html*) to the audio podcast … the link code should be: <bgsound src='Homepage.wav' loop='1'>.

*** How to add a résumé as an internal link

1. Save your résumé as an rtf file (Save as: … 'resume.rtf').

2. Upload the 'resume.rtf' file to the public_html folder.

3. Add a link on your homepage (index.html) to the résumé … the link code is: <ahref='resume.rtf'>Resume</a>

Additional sources

Benedict Visual Literacy Collection, Arizona State University:
   http://www.asu.edu/lib/archives/benedict/index.html
'Campaigning for the Charts that Teach: Talking Numbers with Edward Tufte,' by David Corcoran:
   http://www.edwardtufte.com/tufte/nytimes_0200
'CMC Info: Computer-Mediated Communication Information Sources,' by John December:
   http://www.december.com/cmc/info/
The McLuhan Program in Culture and Technology, University of Toronto, Canada:
   http://www.mcluhan.utoronto.ca/

Marshall McLuhan Global Research Network:
http://www.mcluhan.org/
'Visual Literacy,' by Jamie McKenzie:
http://www.fno.org/PL/vislit.htm
'Why is Visual Literacy Important?':
http://www.museumca.org/picturethis/visual.html

Notes

1. Trent Think Tank on Media Literacy, Ontario, Canada, 1989.
2. California Polytechnic State University, Information Competence Project, at: *http://lib.calpoly.edu/infocomp/* (accessed 7 July 2009).
3. Fred Johnson, Portland State University, 'Digital Literacy: Re-Thinking Education and Training in a Digital World,' at: *http://digitalliteracy.mwg .org* (accessed 7 July 2009).
4. CNN, 'Profile: R.E. "Ted" Turner,' at: *http://archives.cnn.com/2001/ WORLD/europe/04/10/turner.profile/index.html* (accessed 6 March 2009).
5. Who2, 'Robert L. Johnson Biography,' at: *http://www.who2.com/ robertljohnson.html* (accessed 6 March 2009).
6. Investing Value, 'Rupert Murdoch Biography,' at: *http://www.investingvalue .com/investment-leaders/rupert-murdoch/index.htm* (accessed 6 March 2009).
7. Internet Movie Database (IMDB), 'Biography for Matt Drudge,' at: *http:// www.imdb.com/name/nm1002654/bio* (accessed 6 March 2009).
8. Ruth Katz and Elihu Katz (1998) 'McLuhan: where did he come from? Where did he disappear?' *Canadian Journal of Communications*, 23, at: *http://www.cjc-online.ca/index.php/journal/article/view/1046* (accessed 3 May 2009); Marshall McLuhan (1964) *Understanding Media: The Extensions of Man.* New York: McGraw-Hill.
9. International Visual Literacy Association, at: *http://www.ivla.org/* (accessed 7 June 2009).
10. International Visual Literacy Association, 'What is Visual Literacy?' at: *http://www.ivla.org/org_what_vis_lit.htm* (accessed 7 June 2009).
11. 'The Work of Edward Tufte and Graphics Press,' at: *http://www.edwardtufte .com/tufte/* (accessed 7 June 2009).
12. Edward Tufte (1997) *Visual Explanations: Images and Quantities, Evidence and Narrative.* Cheshire, CT: Graphics Press, p. 127, at: *http://www.evl .uic.edu/davidson/CurrentProjects98/ET_VisualInfo/Meta_Principle.html* (accessed 7 June 2009).
13. Ibid., p. 34.
14. Ibid., p. 126.
15. Edward Tufte (1987) *The Visual Display of Quantitative Information.* Cheshire, CT: Graphics Press, p. 141, at: *http://www.evl.uic.edu/davidson/ CurrentProjects98/ET_VisualInfo/3rd_Principle.html* (accessed 7 June 2009).

16. Edward Tufte (1990) *Envisioning Information*. Cheshire, CT: Graphics Press, p. 31, at: *http://www.evl.uic.edu/davidson/CurrentProjects98/ET_VisualInfo/3rd_Principle.html* (accessed 7 June 2009).
17. Ibid., p. 18, at: *http://www.evl.uic.edu/davidson/CurrentProjects98/ET_VisualInfo/5th_Principle.html* (accessed 7 June 2009).
18. Charles Minard, '19th-Century Map of Napoleon's 1812 March into Russia,' at: *http://www.evl.uic.edu/aej/422/GIFs/napoleon.gif* (accessed 7 July 2009).
19. Peter Vinten-Johansen et al. (2003) *Cholera, Chloroform and the Science of Medicine: A Life of John Snow*. Oxford University Press; National Geographic, 'Map of Cholera Deaths,' at: *http://www.nationalgeographic.com/resources/ngo/education/ideas912/912choleraho2.html* (accessed 7 June 2009).

10

Government literacy

Which is the best government? That which teaches us to govern ourselves. (Johann Wolfgang von Goethe)

Early influences on Western governments

Mesopotamia

Scholars consider the *Code of Hammurabi* to be one of the earliest and the best-preserved examples of a ruler proclaiming publicly (on a carved black stone monument, eight feet high) an entire body of laws, arranged in orderly groups, so that all men might read and know what was required of them. Hammurabi ruled Babylon from 1,795 to 1,750 BC and his Code of Laws may be viewed at the Louvre in Paris.[1]

Other early codes of law include the *Code of Ur-Nammu*, ruler of the Sumerian city of UR (*c.*2,060 BC), the Hittite Code of Laws the *Code of the Nesilim* (*c.*1,650–1,500 BC), and *Mosaic Law Code* (traditionally *c.*1,200 BC under Moses).[2]

Ancient Greeks

Democracy is from the Greek *demokratia*, or 'rule of or by the people' from the root word *polis*, meaning 'city' or 'community' – Greek democracy consisted of free male Greek citizens. Greek principles of democracy can be traced back to the sixth century BC and the Athenian ruler Solon. Solon passed laws that protected Athenian citizens from being enslaved or arrested for debt, and granted Greek citizens certain rights.[3]

The influence of Rome

According to a 1934 article by Ames and Montgomery,[4] it is clear that the legacy of Rome and Greece is alive in the architectural styles of many Washington landmarks, government buildings, and monuments. The influence of Rome does not rest with the most obvious visual aspects of the United States and its institutions but rather the legacy of Rome and her predecessor Greece is at the heart of US ideology, a role model so to speak.

This article discusses the role that the Roman Republic, and later the Roman Empire, played for the founding fathers and their Constitution. The authors note that many people assume that our laws come from English laws and to a degree they do; however, at the time the Constitution was written, England was an active monarchy and did not have any voting bodies as it does today. However, England was not the model which the framers of the Constitution used. Of the 55 original members of the Convention which met to discuss the Constitution, more than 31 were lawyers, and of this group, at least 24 went to Princeton, Harvard, Yale, or William and Mary as well as the most reputable schools in England. They were all well versed in Classical history, Classical law and philosophy.

The founding fathers evoked the ideology of the Roman Republic many times, citing statements from Rome's leading political philosophers. The most notable Roman legacy is the principle of the separation of powers, something that was keenly lacking in imperial England. The idea of a system of checks and balances is fully Roman, not English as typically assumed. This system of separation and balance was the key, the founding fathers believed, to ensuring a fair and balanced system, one that would be able to withstand factions and minority groups who sought to push their agenda on to the majority.

The Roman Republic's constitution defined a threefold political power structure, one that executes law, one that creates law, and one that implements law. This is how our political structure is set up today with courts that execute law, congress and other state and federal organizations which create law, and then the police and military units which implement law. The influence of Rome was indeed powerful and, in a sense, the United States today is the living legacy of the Roman Republic and its political ideology. Without the Roman Republic there is a strong likelihood that the US would be vastly different, and possibly not even democratic.

The Magna Carta

The Magna Carta (Latin for 'Great Paper' or 'Great Charter') was an English charter originally issued in 1215. The Magna Carta was a significant early influence on the long historical process that led to the rule of constitutional law. The Magna Carta required the king to renounce certain rights, respect certain legal procedures, and accept that the will of the king could be bound by law. The original Magna Carta may be seen at the British Library in London (*http://www.bl.uk/treasures/magnacarta*).

Freemasons

The next influence is debatable but worth mentioning. The Freemasons are an old organization that grew out of the Medieval Guild of Masons. Freemasonry (or Masonry) is the oldest and largest fraternal organization and is dedicated to the Brotherhood of Man under the Fatherhood of God. There are indications that the Masons are related to (and may have absorbed) the Knights Templar, who date back to the Crusades.

While the Masonic influence over Western governments, particularly the US government, is the subject of heated debate, here are some related facts:

- Many of the founders of the US government were Masons, including George Washington, James Monroe, Benjamin Franklin, John Hancock, Paul Revere, and John Paul Jones.

- The Cornerstone of the National Capitol was laid on 18 September 1793 by George Washington with a Masonic Ceremony.[5]

Examples of Western governments

United Kingdom of Great Britain and Northern Ireland

- *Type of government*: constitutional monarchy.

- *Constitution*: unwritten – partly statute, partly common law and practice.

Branches

- *Executive*: monarchy – Head of State, Her Majesty Queen Elizabeth II (*http://www.royal.gov.uk/*), Prime Minister (*http://www.number10.gov.uk/*), and Cabinet.

- *Legislature*: bicameral Parliament (*http://www.parliament.uk/*) – House of Commons and House of Lords, Scottish Parliament, Welsh National Assembly, and Northern Ireland Assembly.

- *Judiciary*: magistrates' courts, county courts, high courts, appellate courts.

See also:

- *Guide to UK government*: see Direct.gov (*http://www.direct.gov.uk/*).

- *Guide to UK national statistics*: see Statistics.gov (*http://www.statistics.gov.uk/*).

United States of America

- *Type of government*: constitutional federal republic with a strong democratic tradition.

- *Constitution*: written Constitution and Bill of Rights.

Branches

- *Executive*: The President (WhiteHouse.gov).

- *Congress*: bicameral Congress – Senate (*http://senate.gov*) and House of Representatives (*http://house.gov*).

- *Judiciary*: Supreme Court (*http://supremecourtus.gov/*) and district federal courts (*http://www.uscourts.gov/*).

See also:

- Portal to US government information: USA.gov (*http://www.usa.gov/*).

- Portal to US statistical information: Census.gov (*http://www.census.gov*).

- See the 'American History Timeline' by the Smithsonian Institution (*http://www.si.edu/Encyclopedia_SI/nmah/timeline.htm*).

- Definitions from the *CIA World Factbook*:[6]

  - *Constitutional government*. A government by or operating under an authoritative document (constitution) that sets forth the system of fundamental laws and principles that determine the nature, functions, and limits of that government.

  - *Constitutional democracy*. A form of government in which the sovereign power of the people is spelled out in a governing constitution.

– *Federal republic.* A state in which the powers of the central government are restricted and in which the component parts (states, colonies, or provinces) retain a degree of self-government; ultimate sovereign power rests with the voters who choose their governmental representatives.

Exercises

Exercise 1

Take at least *three* of the following quizzes on the various governments of the world. What did you learn that you did not know? What types of questions were the easiest for you?

1. Branches of the US government – see: *http://www.softschools.com/quizzes/social_studies/branches_of_government/quiz344.html.*

2. Women in British politics – see: *http://www.funtrivia.com/trivia-quiz/World/Women-in-British-Politics-272096.html.*

3. British Prime Ministers, Part I – see: *http://www.funtrivia.com/trivia-quiz/World/British-Prime-Ministers-Part-One-276697.html.*

4. US government – see: *http://www.funtrivia.com/trivia-quiz/World/US-Government-268249.html.*

5. European Union – see: *http://www.funtrivia.com/trivia-quiz/World/European-Union-68070.html.*

6. World leaders 2006 – see: *http://www.funtrivia.com/trivia-quiz/World/World-Leader-2006-248085.html.*

Exercise 2

Research the similarities and differences in the UK and US governments. Write a three-paragraph essay in which you compare and contrast the two governments.

Exercise 3

Look up the requirements for becoming a citizen of the US and the UK.

1. What are the requirements for each?
2. Do you have to take a test?

3. How long does the process take?
4. How are the processes similar?
5. How are they different?

Additional sources

AmericanRevolution.org:
http://americanrevolution.org/home.html
The Royal Exalted Religious and Military Order of Masonic Knights Templar of England and Wales:
http://www.brad.ac.uk/webofhiram/?section=masonic_knights_templar
US government resources by RefDesk.com:
http://www.refdesk.com/factgov.html
Information on each state government as well as the federal government:
http://www.govengine.com
'Toward the City on a Hill: A Brief History of the U.S.':
http://usa.usembassy.de/etexts/factover/ch3.htm

Notes

1. L.W. King (trans.), *Yale Library Avalon Project*, 'The Code of Hammurabi,' at: *http://avalon.law.yale.edu/ancient/hamframe.asp* (accessed 8 March 2009).
2. Boston University School of Theology, List of Ancient Legal Codes, at: *http://sthweb.bu.edu/index.php?option=com_awiki&view=mediawiki&article=List_of_ancient_legal_codes&Itemid=175* (accessed 8 March 2009).
3. Robert K. Fleck and F. Andrew Hanssen (2006) 'The origins of democracy: a model with application to Ancient Greece,' *Journal of Law and Economics*, 49: 115–46.
4. R.A. Ames and Henry C. Montgomery (1934) 'The influence of Rome on the American Constitution,' *Classical Journal*, 30(1): 19–27 (article summary by Leslie Hawkins, 30 August 2006).
5. Guy M. Chalmers, 'Masonic Leaders in the U.S. and Their Influence, 1900–1999,' at: *http://www.calodges.org/ncrl/archive/GMC01.pdf* (accessed 24 June 2009).
6. Central Intelligence Agency, *CIA World Factbook*, at: *https://www.cia.gov/library/publications/the-world-factbook/* (accessed 24 June 2009).

11

Financial literacy

The number one problem in today's generation and economy is the lack of financial literacy. (Alan Greenspan)

If you want to create wealth, it is imperative that you believe that you are at the steering wheel of life, especially your financial life. (T. Harv Eker)

What is financial literacy?

Financial literacy was defined by a 2000 Fannie Mae Foundation report as the ability to read, analyze, manage, and communicate about the personal financial conditions that affect material well-being. Financial literacy includes the ability to discern financial choices, discuss money and financial issues without (or despite) discomfort, plan for the future, and respond competently to life events that affect everyday financial decisions, including events in the general economy.[1]

Financial literacy research and statistics

- Every two years since 1997, the Jump$tart Coalition of Washington, DC has been administering a national financial literacy survey to high-school seniors.[2] Overall, the surveys have indicated a low level of financial literacy: on average, the students correctly answered only half of the questions on a basic personal finance and economics test.[3]

- IndexCreditCards.com used government debt and census data to determine that as of July 2009 the average credit card debt in the United States was $7,861 per household and $4,013 per adult.[4]

What is a credit report?

If you have used a credit card or borrowed money then you have a credit report and a FICO (Fair Isaac Corporation) Credit Score.[5]

A credit score, a number typically between 300 and 850 based on a statistical analysis of one's credit history, indicates the creditworthiness of a person. FICO scores consist of data on the amount of debt you owe, your payment history, the length of your credit history (how long it has been since you first established credit), the amount of new credit you have, and the types of credit you have (credit cards, retail accounts, mortgage, and financial aid). The majority of your credit score (approximately 65 percent) is based on your payment history and the amount of debt that you owe. Information not included in your FICO score includes factors such as your race, where you live, your salary, your occupation, and any other information not typically found in a credit report. The lower the FICO score, the more interest you will pay because those with a low FICO score are considered a higher credit risk. To improve your credit score, pay bills on time and do not run up a huge debt. Check out other tips for improving your FICO score at: *http://www.myfico.com/CreditEducation/ImproveYourScore.aspx*.

You may request a free credit report once every 12 months from each of the nationwide consumer credit reporting companies: Equifax, Experian, and TransUnion at *http://www.annualcreditreport.com* in the US and *http://www.annualcreditreport.co.uk/* in the UK. If any of the reports contain inaccurate information, contact the company immediately and persistently until they correct the inaccuracies.

Compound interest

Unlike simple interest, compound interest is paying interest on the principal *and* interest – in other words, paying interest on top of interest over time. With regard to compound interest, Albert Einstein is quoted as saying, 'It is the greatest mathematical discovery of all time.'[6]

Einstein is also credited with discovering the compound interest Rule of 72 (*http://ruleof72.net*):

- To find out the number of years it would take to double your money at various interest rates, take the number 72 and divide it by the interest rate. For example, if you wanted to invest $1,000 at 20 percent interest, you would earn $360 in interest per year. Thus it would take you two and a half years to double your money.

- To find out the interest rate you would need to double your money within a certain period of time, take the number 72 and divide by the number of years you want to invest. For example, if you invested $2,000 and wanted to double your money in five years, you would divide 72 by 5, which is 14.4. Thus you could double your money in five years with an interest rate of 14.4 percent.

If you are saving money in an interest-paying account such as a savings account, then you are earning compound interest. If you keep a balance on a credit card, you are paying compound interest. For example, if you have a credit card debt of $7,500 at 10 percent interest and you want to pay it off in five years, you would owe $13,217.56. Thus you would owe $5,717.56 in interest. To calculate the amount of interest you would pay on a credit card, go to *http://math.about.com/library/blcompoundinterest.htm*.

The secret to financial success is to avoid paying compound interest while being paid compound interest.

Financial resources

Resources for financial literacy

ControlYourCredit.gov:
  http://controlyourcredit.gov/
Grad Guide to the Real World:
  http://finance.yahoo.com/college-education/article/103030/Grad-Guide-to-the-Real-World
Debt Diet:
  http://www.oprah.com/article/money/debt/20080722_expert_debtdietsteps

Resources for student scholarships

'Smart Student Guide to Financial Aid':
  http://www.finaid.org/scholarships/
Federal student aid:
  http://www.fafsa.ed.gov/
Scholarship opportunities:
  http://www.scholarshiphelp.org/

Exercises

Exercise 1

Find a career – look in the *Occupational Outlook Handbook* (*http://www.bls.gov/OCO/*) and search for your future profession.

1. What is the job outlook in your field?
2. What is the median salary in your field?
3. How much money per month do you think you will need to support yourself and will this salary give you what you need?

Exercise 2

Create an imaginary budget in an Excel spreadsheet. Create a salary as large as you would wish to have upon graduation:

1. Title the spreadsheet at the bottom.
2. Label two columns monthly and yearly; format with the multiplication formula in the yearly column to automatically multiply each monthly column by 12.
3. Label rows for each of the following expenditure categories:
   - a payroll tax deduction of about 40 percent;
   - payment for yourself – budget at least 10 percent for savings;
   - 10 percent for charity is suggested;
   - mortgage or rent (usually about one week or one-quarter of a month's salary), transportation (vehicle, gas, insurance, or public transport), utilities (electricity, gas, water), food;
   - a category for clothes and personal grooming and another category for gifts and miscellaneous.
4. Highlight the numerical figures in each column and click on the sigma icon (Σ) to total each column at the bottom.
5. Create a pie chart to illustrate your budget.

Exercise 3

Keep track of expenses. For one week, keep a diary of every penny that is spent each day.

1. What is the total for each day?

2. What is the total for the week? What is the average per day?

3. What are the most expensive items per week?

4. Make a list of free or low-cost substitutes for five of the items on your list. How much money could you save each week? How much would that be per year?

Additional sources

Financial privacy resources:
> *http://www.privacyrights.org/financial.htm*

MyMoney.gov from the US Financial Literacy & Education Commission has a wealth of information related to financial literacy:
> *http://mymoney.gov*

To learn how to get out of debt, check out the Dave Ramsey website (*http://www.daveramsey.com/*) or one of his books, such as *Financial Peace* (2002).

To learn how to live well for less and how to stretch your resources, check out the Clark Howard website (*http://clarkhoward.com/*) or one of his books, such as *Get Clark Smart* (2002).

Notes

1. Lois Vitt et al. (2000) *Personal Finance and the Rush to Competence: Financial Literacy Education in the U.S.*, Fannie Mae Foundation, Middleburg, VA, at: *http://www.isfs.org/rep_finliteracy.pdf* (accessed 21 June 2009).

2. Jump$tart Coalition for Personal Financial Literacy – see: *http://www.jumpstartcoalition.org/* (accessed 21 June 2009).

3. Lewis Mandell (2005) 'Financial Literacy: Does It Matter?' University of Buffalo, 8 April, at: *http://www.vajumpstart.org/files/Mandell%20Paper%20April%202005.doc* (accessed 21 June 2009).

4. IndexCreditCards.com, 'Credit Card Debt,' at: *http://www.indexcreditcards.com/creditcarddebt/* (accessed 21 July 2009).

5. Credit score information – MyFICO, at: *http://www.myfico.com/CreditEducation/CreditScores.aspx* (accessed 21 June 2009).

6. Albert Einstein: the rule of 72 – see: *http://www.ruleof72.net/rule-of-72-einstein.asp* (accessed 21 June 2009).

12

Writing a research paper

Research is formalized curiosity. It is poking and prying with a purpose. (Zora Neale Hurston)

There is nothing like looking, if you want to find something. You certainly usually find something, if you look, but it is not always quite the something you were after. (J.R.R. Tolkien)

Writing in general may be categorized into two basic types: *informal* and *formal*:

- Informal writing includes personal accounts and reflective journals and blogs; the informal style of writing includes the use of contractions and personal pronouns.
- Formal writing includes scholarly research papers and reports; the formal style requires an objective tone and an avoidance of contractions and personal pronouns.

How does one begin to write a formal research paper?

The first step in writing a formal paper is to determine the *type of paper* and the *topic*. There are two basic types of research paper:

- In an *argumentative research* paper the author writes a thesis statement then text that builds a case for the thesis in a persuasive manner.
- In an *analytical research* paper an author uses research questions or hypotheses to investigate a research problem in an objective manner.[1]

Topic selection

The next step is topic selection. Some factors to think about are:

- What interests you?
- What topic would be useful in your future career?

Another strategy is to browse some scholarly journals in the relevant field, browse a scholarly database, or talk to a subject specialist such as an academic professor or a reference librarian.

Selecting sources

Once the topic is selected, it is time to search for scholarly sources. Typically, an academic research paper should use several types of sources including journals, books, encyclopedias, newspapers, and perhaps some websites.

- Reference works, particularly subject encyclopedias and dictionaries, can provide background information for the introduction.
- Peer-reviewed research articles from scholarly academic journals can provide the most reliable sources for the paper.
- Scholarly books may provide in-depth information.
- Websites may provide statistics, organizational information and other information.

Search terms

- Once the topic is identified, list the terms and concepts that describe the topic.
- These terms will become the keywords used to search library catalogs, indexes, and databases for information on the topic.

Research topic example

As stated in Chapter 5, it is advisable to have at least one source for every page of content in the paper. For example, for a 20-page paper, you would want to have at least 20 sources. You may not use all of your sources, but it is better to have a few too many sources than to have too few and have to scramble to find more at the last minute.

- *Topic*: Alzheimer's disease in women.
- *Keywords*: dementia, cognition disorders, brain, senior citizens.

Outlining the paper

Once you have located and read the relevant sources gathered for the paper, think about the various subtopics or areas that will be included in the paper. First brainstorm and list all the subjects related to the topic of the paper, then use this list to construct an outline of headings and subheadings for the paper. This will help you organize the paper in a logical manner. After the outline is done, work on one section at a time. When the paper is complete, proofread for errors and to check for logical flow and consistency. This is a good time to re-read the paper instructions to be sure they were followed and to have a friend or colleague proofread the paper and give you feedback.

Grammar checklist

1. Do not use contractions in formal or scholarly writing, *especially* when writing formal reports or research papers.

2. Possessive *its* is not a contraction and does not contain an apostrophe.

3. Do use bulleted lists in scholarly writing to improve readability.

4. Be sure that items in a bulleted list or a listing in a sentence all begin with *the same part of speech*, e.g. noun, verb, adjective, adverb. Using this method is an example of *parallelism*.

5. Use two spaces after periods, colons, and question marks when writing scholarly letters and documents.

6. Be sure an independent clause precedes a colon. However, lists introduced by a *verb* should not have a colon.

7. Personal pronouns may be used in reflective, informal writing but avoid using first-person or second-person pronouns in scholarly or formal documents. These documents should have an objective tone and use third-person pronouns.

   - First person pronouns include the words *I, me, my, we, our.*
   - Second person pronouns include the words *you, your.*
   - Third person pronouns include the words *he, she, they, their, him, her, it.*

8. Avoid ending sentences with prepositions, e.g. 'Where is the meeting at?'

9. Use a comma with the word *which* in a sentence as this word introduces non-essential information; do not use commas with the word *that* as this word introduces essential information.

10. Capitalize proper nouns that are names of specific persons, places, or things. Do not capitalize words that are not proper nouns. Use italics or underlining for placing special emphasis on words.

11. Within the text of a document, enclose article titles in quotation marks; book or journal titles should be underlined or in italics. Acronyms of journal titles should also be underlined or in italics (*JASIS*).

12. *Internet* is now a proper noun and should be capitalized; e-mail and e-journal are not capitalized.

13. Use an en dash (not a hyphen) to denote the term *through*, e.g. (1999–2000).

14. The words *thank you* should be hyphenated when followed by a noun, e.g. thank-you note. (Rule: Two adjectives preceding a noun are hyphenated, e.g. all-important fact.)

15. Use appropriate in-text references; include page number(s) for a direct or indirect quote.

16. Be careful about subject–verb agreement, particularly with Latin words: datum is singular, data are plural; medium is singular, media are plural; analysis is singular, analyses are plural; criterion is singular, criteria are plural; thesis is singular, theses are plural; hypothesis is singular, hypotheses are plural.

17. Tables (data in columns and rows) and figures (charts, graphs, images) should be appropriately numbered and titled (capitalize major words in title) and should be referenced in the text (Table 1).

18. When creating tables, remember that numbers are right-aligned and text is left-aligned.[2]

Research paper format

The research paper format varies according to the discipline and the professor's instructions, but below is one example of the required format for an analytical paper.

[Research paper title page format: an appropriate title for the paper should be centered with major words capitalized.]

Research Paper Title

Student Name
E-mail address

Course Number
Date

[Research paper body format: distinguish between topic headings and subtopics/subheadings; for example, center main topics or headings, left-align subtopics/subheadings.]

Introduction

Background information about the topic of the study and importance of the study. (The importance of the study may come at the beginning or the end of the introduction section.)

Purpose of the study

Clear, concise and focused purpose of the study: the problem statement including sub-problems.

Research questions or *hypotheses*

Clearly state the specific research questions *or* hypotheses. Choose one but *not* both. Use the present tense and number appropriately: R1, R2, etc. for research questions; H1, H2, etc, for hypotheses.

Definitions

List relevant terms or acronyms and their definitions. Properly cite the source(s) of the definitions.

Limitations and delimitations of the study

State what is included in the study and what is excluded from the study.

Assumptions

State the assumptions embedded in the research design.

Importance of the study

End the introduction section with a statement about the importance of the study unless this is addressed in the introductory paragraphs.

Literature review

The literature review paints the background for the research, creating a frame of reference and context. Research builds upon previous research so it is important to recognize and credit previous studies that are similar in topic and methodology.

Use subtopics if appropriate. Some topics have a previous body of research that is related to the topic *and* methodology but students may find research related to the topic and other studies that use the same or similar methodology but few or no previous studies that use the same methodology to study the same topic. In this instance, it is appropriate to have a subtopic on studies related to the subject or topic of the study and another subtopic related to studies that use the same methodology as this study on similar topics.

Subtopics should follow a logical flow. For instance, when reviewing the studies that use a particular methodology, it would be useful to put them in chronological order within that subtopic to indicate a progression of the research that leads up to this research.

Each review of a scholarly study should include a summary of the methodology and results. It should be clear to the reader how each study reviewed is related to this study. End with a concluding paragraph about how this study is similar to or different from the studies reviewed.

Methodology

Begin the methodology section with a description of the methodology used in this study. Include details of data sources, how appropriate data are identified, and data collection procedures (detailed enough so that it could be replicated by others). State how data are compiled and analyzed, including software used such as Word tables or Excel. (For a *research proposal*, the methodology should be written in the future tense; for a final *research report*, the methodology should be changed to the past tense).

Results

Restate each research question *or* hypothesis (these may be used as subheadings), then the results of the data analysis. Research questions are answered or addressed; hypotheses are tested and supported or not supported by the data (do *not* use the word 'prove'). It is desirable to use tables (data in columns and rows) and figures (charts, graphs, images) to illustrate data analysis. Each table or figure should be appropriately titled and numbered and referenced in the text ('see Table 1'). Tables or figures longer than three-quarters of a page may be placed at the end of the paper as an appendix and referenced appropriately in the text ('see Appendix'). If the study is a survey, include the survey instrument as an appendix. Number appendices if there is more than one ('see Appendix 1'). Data in tables or figures may be single-spaced or 1½ spaced. Journal or book titles in tables or figures should be italicized or underlined just as in the text.

Discussion

Summarize and discuss the research results. Compare the results with the results of previous studies reviewed in the literature review. Discuss *possible* general conclusions (using cautious language) that may be drawn from the study results. End with a concluding paragraph that suggests further research related to this study.

Bibliography (or References or Works cited)

List citations of works referenced in the paper in chronological order by author. Use the required citation style (or the style of your choice if permitted) and be consistent.

Additional formatting requirements

- Insert page numbers but do not number the first, title page.
- Generally, double-space *or* single-space with an extra space between paragraphs (be sure to follow specific instructions).
- Parenthetical references should be within the sentence, before the ending punctuation (Welsh, 2009).
- Include page number when referencing direct or indirect quotes. Use *n.p.* (no page) if there is no page number (Wright, 2009, n.p.).
- A research proposal includes the Introduction section, Literature Review section, and Methodology section written in the future tense. For the completed research report, change the tense in the Methodology to past tense, and add the Results section and Discussion section.
- Be sure there is consistency and logical flow to the research report. Do the methodology, results and conclusion 'match' or address the introduction and problem statement? Is it clear to the reader what research this study builds upon and how it builds upon that research? Could the reader replicate this study?

- Avoid using superlative, overly definitive language, such as best, most, very, etc.; instead, use cautious language; for example, 'results indicate' … or 'data indicate.'
- Review the 'grammar checklist' for correct grammar usage in formal scholarly papers.

For examples of scholarly bibliometric research papers, see Appendices 2, 3, and 4.

Additional sources

OASIS (Online Advancement of Student Information Skills) Tutorial: *http://oasis.sfsu.edu/*
'Outlines: How They Can Improve Your Writing,' by Dr Dennis G. Jerz: *http://jerz.setonhill.edu/writing/academic/outline.htm*
'Selecting Resources,' by Duke Libraries: *http://library.duke.edu/services/instruction/libraryguide/*
Selecting sources quiz: *http://regisnet.regiscollege.edu/library/infolit/selsoquiz.htm*
'The Seven Steps of the Research Process,' by Cornell Libraries: *http://www.library.cornell.edu/olinuris/ref/research/skill1.htm*

Notes

1. Purdue University, Online Writing Lab (OWL): *http://owl.english.purdue.edu/* (accessed 24 June 2009).
2. Adapted from a Grammar Checklist by Dr LaJuan Davis for the Southern Mississippi Quality Enhancement Program (QEP) Faculty Seminar, October 2008.

13

Conclusion

Information literacy may be defined as the ability to find, locate, and evaluate current, relevant, and accurate information and to use this information effectively in order to meet one's needs. A generation ago, most information was found using the newspaper, television, radio, or scholarly journals which could be located using a library card catalog or the *Reader's Guide to Periodical Literature*. While these media are still used, much information can now be found using computers and the Internet. The current generation of college students is the first to grow up immersed in technology and the Internet. They are often referred to as 'Web 2.0 students,' 'the Net Generation,' or 'Digital Natives.'[1]

By the age of 21, the average person of this generation 'will have spent 10,000 hours playing video games, 20,000 watching television, 10,000 hours on his/her cell phone, and [sent and received] 200,000 e-mails.'[2] However, they will have spent less than 5,000 hours reading. Therefore, while the definition of information literacy is still accurate, the ways in which it is accessed and used have changed drastically. Users now often rely on the Internet, social networking sites such as Facebook or MySpace, Web 2.0 software such as Twitter, and blogs to meet their information needs. The focus of teaching information literacy skills, then, needs to be not only on finding needed information, but especially on evaluating the content and the creators of online digital content for accuracy and currency.

Top tips for evaluating information on the Web

1. Determine who wrote it. Are the authors' names, affiliation, and contact information listed on the website?

Reason: The more information that is provided about the authors or creators of a website, the more one will be able to assess their qualifications for writing about the topic. In addition, one may be able to contact the author to ask for clarification or to inquire about other sources of information related to the topic.

2. Determine how current the information is. Can you find when the information was last updated? If the information is about technology, medicine, science, or geography, look for information that is less than five years old.

   Reason: Information that is too dated can be incorrect. For example, if a person were to look at a map of the world produced before 1989, he/she would find that Germany was two countries (East and West Germany), rather than one.

3. Determine the accuracy of the information. Determine whether or not the information can be verified in at least two other sources. Look for reference or citation lists for the content of the website.

   Reason: Incorrect information can lead to mistakes being made in research experiments or people being misinformed and possibly making incorrect decisions.

4. Avoid information which contains many grammatical, punctuation, and spelling errors.

   Reason: If the authors or creators of a website do not take the time to ensure that the content contains few grammatical or spelling errors, they may not take the time to ensure that the information is accurate.

5. Avoid using sources such as Wikipedia where anyone can contribute information.

   Reason: In sources such as Wikipedia, anyone, regardless of their credentials and/or qualifications, may contribute content on any subject. This could easily lead to incorrect or inaccurate information being presented.

6. Determine if the authors or creators of a website have any biases.

   Reason: Biases could result in a one-sided point of view of the topic being discussed. Thus people reading the information may not receive balanced or complete coverage of an issue.

7. Determine if there are broken links to other websites. If there are too many broken links, another source should be used.

   Reason: Broken links tend to indicate that the information may be outdated.

8. Determine the clarity of the information. A college or university undergraduate student should be able to read and clearly understand the content.

   Reason: If the information is presented in such a way that it is too difficult to read or comprehend, it is much more difficult to understand what is being presented and thus evaluate it for accuracy.

9. Is the website easily accessible with little animation and a site map?

   Reason: Good information is good information. It doesn't need fancy animation which detracts from it. A site map is necessary for good organization. If the information is not well organized and easy to access, it really doesn't matter how good it is.

Important note about digital e-content: *do not assume that e-content such as text messages, mobile phone images, social networking sites, or websites are private*. E-content is usually archived on at least one server and usually on multiple servers, and can easily be copied or forwarded. So do not put anything online or in a text message that you would not want in the public domain.

Notes

1. D. Rosen and C. Nelson (2008) 'Web 2.0: a new generation of learners and education,' *Computers in the Schools*, 25(3–4): 211–25.
2. A. Bonamici, D. Hutto, D. Smith, and J. Ward (2005) *The 'Net Generation': Implications for Libraries and Higher Education*. Presentation at the Orbis Cascade Alliance Council Meeting, Bellingham, WA.

Appendix 1
Information Competency Assessment Instrument

Directions: This instrument is composed of 40 statements concerning feelings about finding and disseminating research information. Please indicate the degree to which each statement applies to you by circling the number that best fits your feelings on the statement from whether you (1) strongly disagree to (7) strongly agree. Using the following scale, please record your first impression.

1	2	3	4	5	6	7
strongly disagree			neither agree or disagree			strongly agree

1.	I feel confident determining what topic I need to search.	1	2	3	4	5	6	7
2.	Sometimes I feel lost because the topic I want to research is not very clear to me.	1	2	3	4	5	6	7
3.	I can take a complex topic and break it down into more useful, simpler items.	1	2	3	4	5	6	7
4.	'Confused' is probably the best term to describe me when starting a project.	1	2	3	4	5	6	7
5.	I am sometimes unsure of how much information I need for the assignment.	1	2	3	4	5	6	7
6.	I know the difference between 'primary' and 'secondary' sources.	1	2	3	4	5	6	7
7.	I get confused because of the many different formats (print, electronic, etc.) when searching for information.	1	2	3	4	5	6	7
8.	I am certain that I can use the information I find.	1	2	3	4	5	6	7

9.	I know how to broaden or narrow a search using Boolean operators (AND, NOT and OR) and truncation.	1 2 3 4 5 6 7
10.	It is easy to interpret the results of a search.	1 2 3 4 5 6 7
11.	I'm not sure how to use an index (e.g. catalog, database, etc.).	1 2 3 4 5 6 7
12.	I can confidently get my hands on the material (by printing, e-mailing, interlibrary loan, etc.) I need.	1 2 3 4 5 6 7
13.	I understand the organization of materials in libraries.	1 2 3 4 5 6 7
14.	Government documents are confusing to me.	1 2 3 4 5 6 7
15.	Web search engines are unreliable.	1 2 3 4 5 6 7
16.	I know the difference between an abstract and an article.	1 2 3 4 5 6 7
17.	Sometimes I cannot figure out for whom the information is intended.	1 2 3 4 5 6 7
18.	I can use many different types of media (print, video, photography, etc.) confidently as information for my topic.	1 2 3 4 5 6 7
19.	At times, the producer of the information is not clear.	1 2 3 4 5 6 7
20.	I can confidently spot inaccuracy, errors, etc. in the information from mass media.	1 2 3 4 5 6 7
21.	The information I find is so confusing that I don't know if I can use it.	1 2 3 4 5 6 7
22.	I am not confident that the information I get is accurate.	1 2 3 4 5 6 7
23.	The information I use is complete and reliable.	1 2 3 4 5 6 7
24.	I am sure that the information I have answers my question or addresses my topic.	1 2 3 4 5 6 7
25.	A lot of the information I find is irrelevant or unnecessary.	1 2 3 4 5 6 7
26.	After collecting my information, it is easy to sort by content that is similar.	1 2 3 4 5 6 7
27.	Sometimes my question changes depending on what information I find.	1 2 3 4 5 6 7
28.	If my topical outline doesn't make sense, I get discouraged.	1 2 3 4 5 6 7
29.	I am *not* sure which communication medium (transparencies, slides, video, etc.) is appropriate for the delivery of this information.	1 2 3 4 5 6 7

30.	I know my audience and that the information I present meets their needs.	1	2	3	4	5	6	7
31.	I sometimes have doubts as to why I am communicating this information.	1	2	3	4	5	6	7
32.	I am confident that my information is clearly and confidently presented.	1	2	3	4	5	6	7
33.	I'm not sure how to record or cite all my sources.	1	2	3	4	5	6	7
34.	I have questions about the privacy of the information I receive.	1	2	3	4	5	6	7
35.	I can tell when information is biased.	1	2	3	4	5	6	7
36.	I know when material is confidential, should not be used.	1	2	3	4	5	6	7
37.	While preparing a project, I am certain how it will be received by others.	1	2	3	4	5	6	7
38.	Feedback is demoralizing to me.	1	2	3	4	5	6	7
39.	I am able to learn what processes would be helpful for finding information in the future.	1	2	3	4	5	6	7
40.	After the presentation of the information, I'm not sure how it was received.	1	2	3	4	5	6	7

Source: Rodney Marshall (2006) 'An instrument to measure information competency', *Journal of Literacy and Technology: An Academic Journal*. Online at: *http://www.literacyandtechnology.org/volume7/marshallJLT2006.pdf*.

Appendix 2
Information Literacy Assessment Trial Study of Students in the 11th Grade in Mississippi

Janet Boswell, University of Southern Mississippi,
August 16, 2007

This trial study assessed information literacy skills of Mississippi High School Students in the 11th grade and sought to compare the information gathered in schools having low accreditation ratings with those with high accreditation ratings to reveal possible discrepancies. A free, multiple-choice, web-based evaluation instrument based on literacy standards developed by the American Association of School Librarians (AASL), a division of the American Library Association (ALA), was administered to a selection of college-bound students from participating high schools in the state. An evaluation report was generated by the software program and scrutinized for information literacy (IL) deficiencies and by school performance levels.

Background

In 1989 a Final Report was released by the Presidential Committee on Information Literacy that laid out challenges and needs for information literacy in today's society. The report viewed information literacy as absolutely necessary in our current society for people to participate effectively in business and the democratic way of life. Schools were charged with promoting equality for all citizens by creating programs that taught young people how to seek out appropriate information, evaluate sources for bias and authenticity, and effectively use and communicate data (ALA, 1989).

Almost a decade later, *A Progress Report on Information Literacy: An Update on the American Library Association Presidential Committee on Information Literacy: Final Report* was released (ALA, 1998). This report noted progress and provided recommendations on information literacy efforts for the future and reiterated the importance of the ability of citizens to recognize the need for information, to locate appropriate sources, and to use and communicate the information effectively in a world where information is increasing at an unprecedented rate. Emphasis in this report was placed on the need for investments in technology and in all types of educational programs that teach information literacy. An example of progress stated in this report was the establishment of the National Forum on Information Literacy. The update also revealed that in 1994–95 a national survey was administered to measure information literacy levels in 3,236 accredited post-secondary institutions. This report encouraged the Forum to continue to promote and track progress on information literacy. A further recommendation was that 'State Departments of Education, Commissions on Higher Education and Academic Governing Boards should be responsible to ensure that a climate conducive to students becoming information literate exists in their states and on their campuses' (ALA, 1998: 2).

The considerable amount of information giving educators ideas about ways to approach teaching literacy skills to students – instructional web pages, tutorials, etc. – gives evidence of the awareness of the importance placed on the acquisition of information literacy skills. Institutions of higher learning expect prospective students to have literacy skills that can be honed during the years in which students are enrolled at a college or university. However, to be information literate, people must be able to seek out, evaluate, and use information for their business and personal use when formal education is done. It is imperative in this information-rich society to become a productive citizen.

The question then becomes why is measurement of these admittedly important skills lacking – especially in secondary schools? Bonnie Gratch Lindauer and colleagues in their article 'The Three Arenas of Information Literacy Assessment' suggests that lack of expertise, lack of time and lack of financial and/or human resources may be some reasons why this phase of the instructional process is neglected in higher education institutions (2004: 122). It may reasonably be assumed that these problems also exist at the secondary level as well, in addition to the challenges presented by time-constraining curriculum mandates.

The charge then appears clear to educators. Information literacy is vital, being able to measure information literacy is equally important, and in a teaching environment constrained by time, money, and resources, educators must seek ways of teaching and assessing information literacy.

A newly developed instrument funded by the Institute of Museum and Library Services (IMLS) and the United States Department of Education – Tool for Real-time Assessment of Information Literacy Skills (TRAILS) – addresses this issue at the secondary school level. Finished for use in the 2005–06 school year but still ripe for modification as more data become available, this instrument was developed by the Libraries and Media Services (LMS) at Kent State University in Ohio. The project director is Barbara F. Schloman, PhD, AHIP, Associate Dean and Professor, Libraries & Media Services at Kent State University. Based on Ohio state standards for information literacy and standards described in *Information Power: Building Partnerships for Learning*, the purpose of the project was to 'foster collaboration between teachers and librarians who are concerned with advancing library and information literacy in the PK-12 school curriculum' (online, TRAILS, *http://www.trails9.org/*). More specifically the web-based, multiple choice evaluation instrument seeks to 'identify strengths and weaknesses in the information-seeking skills of their students' (online, TRAILS, *http://www.trails9.org/*).

Problem statement

The research problem propelling this project was: 'How well developed are the information-seeking skills of students in Mississippi?' Sub-problems include how well 11th grade students perform on an information literacy assessment, in what areas they are deficient, and whether there are differences in schools with different accreditation ratings. This study evaluated questionnaires answered by 11th grade students in the state of Mississippi in the spring of 2007.

Research questions

1. How well do the 11th grade students in this study perform on the TRAILS Information Literacy Quiz?
2. If students lack literacy skills, in what skills are they deficient?
3. Do students in schools with lower accreditation ratings lack literacy skills possessed by students in higher-rated schools?

Definitions

Information literacy – 'To be information literate, a person must be able to recognize when information is needed and have the ability to locate, evaluate and use effectively the needed information' (definition from the Final Report of the American Library Association (ALA) Presidential Committee on Information Literacy (1989: 1)).

Limitations/delimitations

Since Mississippi has no specifically defined state standards, as confirmed by Rhonda Smith, Foreign Language/Library Media Specialist for the Mississippi Department of Education (personal communication, March 20, 2007), the general literacy standards set forth by the AASL are used for the state standards and for the purpose of this research project. These standards are listed in the Mississippi School Library Media Guide (2002: 18–20). The TRAILS assessments do not test the AASL standards that deal with students' appreciation of literature and creative expression and how the student contributes information to the learning community, sharing and collaborating with others.

This study was limited to a sample of students from five public high schools in Mississippi. The results may not be generalized to the entire state of Mississippi. The site coordinator at each school was charged with selecting students and survey administration. Differences in ability levels, homogeneous or heterogeneous groupings of students, site facilities or method of survey administration may influence the ability to compare groups effectively.

Assumptions

The assumption was made for this project that computer access would be available in each school. Since then Mississippi Governor Ronnie Musgrove mandated in 2001 that every classroom in Mississippi would have a computer connected to the Internet.

It was assumed that the teacher or librarian appointed as site coordinator in each participating school would have technological skills sufficient to administer the survey and collect and report the data for that school and that principals would receive and respond to an e-mail invitation to participate in this project.

Importance of study

This pilot study may be indicative of information literacy strengths and weaknesses of 11th grade students in Mississippi. Results of this study may help target specific information literacy deficiencies and may be used as a tool to develop better information literacy teaching resources.

Literature review

Information literacy standards prepared by the AASL are published in Chapter 2 of *Information Power: Building Partnerships for Learning*. These literacy skills dovetail into the Information Literacy Competency Standards for Higher Education approved by the Association of College and Research Libraries (ACRL) in 2000. The body of literature suggesting ways that information specialists may address and improve information literacy has grown in the last decade; however, evaluation instruments to measure what students actually know are relatively rare and difficult to locate.

Information literacy in secondary schools

These papers and publications, however, oriented towards the university environment, often are more complex than is either necessary or useful for the K-12 librarian. In 1989, the American Library Association in its *Presidential Committee on Information Literacy: Final Report*, stated that 'no K-12 report has explored the potential role of libraries or the need for information literacy' (p. 4). The report went on to envision what an Information Age school might look like and recommended efforts towards information literacy. In 1998, the ALA issued an update to the 1989 report noting progress made on the initial recommendation and efforts made by other organizations, and made further recommendations as the definition of information literacy was better defined and the challenges more clearly seen. Also in 1998, the American Association of School Librarians and the Association for Educational Communications and Technology published *Information Power: Building Partnerships for Learning*, which defined a very detailed set of standards for K-12 information literacy, including examples for various content areas. This report defined nine information literacy standards with accompanying levels of proficiency, and 'Standards In Action' for each grade level grouping (K–2, 3–5, 6–8, 9–12) (pp. 9–43). It further established goals and principles for educators to allow students to reach the nine standards (pp. 59–115).

Information Literacy Competency Standards for Higher Education (2000), published by the Association of College and Research Libraries, delineates five standards and 22 competencies of information literacy, and notes that these provide 'higher education an opportunity to articulate its information literacy competencies with those of K-12' (p. 5), but the report does not itself delineate the differences. Street (2005), addressing the necessity of including the Internet and other electronic resources in current events assignments by social studies teachers, wrote of the need for secondary school teachers to help students develop 'habits of mind' (p. 271) that would better prepare them for college and career. He contended that 'it is vital that teachers equip students with the "habits of mind" necessary for them to evaluate Web-based resources critically. This is especially compelling because of the rapid evolution of new technologies used by adolescents to communicate in and out of school' (p. 271). As information literacy became an issue in the educational community and society as a whole, there was some debate over if and where it should be taught.

Peter Levine (2005) noted that '(s)ome people may feel that improving one's research skills is primarily one's personal responsibility, not a job for public schools' (Levine, 2005: Why Schools Should Play a Role Section, para. 26). However, he said, '(s)chools are often asked to address problems that have implications for the common welfare as well as personal well-being. Online misinformation is a good example of such a problem' (Levine, 2005: Why Schools Should Play a Role Section, para. 26), and '(a)nother traditional purpose of public schooling is to reduce economic and social inequality by increasing the skills of less advantaged people. The World Wide Web may exacerbate existing inequalities: people who are information literate and have Internet connections can glean valuable free information, but those without skills or access to the Internet cannot' (Levine, 2005: Why Schools Should Play a Role Section, para. 29). He notes that, increasingly, in our everyday lives we must learn more about topics like health care that once would have been left to the experts, and that new media and information sources can provide much needed information if the source is trustworthy.

In 2003, Ercegovac explored ways of increasing collaboration between secondary school librarians and their counterparts in higher education. He described some potential barriers to collaboration, including lack of room in the school curricula, and a lack of willingness to give up 'intellectual space to library instruction' (p. 78). Possible remedies to this reluctance are forming teacher-librarian partnerships in middle school, where the curriculum is more flexible, and in social studies rather than science classes, where lab activities 'often overpower those in libraries' (p. 78).

Smalley (2004) found that '(a)cross the entire educational spectrum, librarians are aware that teaching information literacy skills is an important component to educational success' (p. 193) in her research detailing the connection between the availability and quality of information literacy education and student performance in college. Comparing results at Cabrillo College, she found a clear correlation in post-secondary achievement between students from schools with no librarians and students from schools with librarians in three California school districts (p. 195). Melissa Gross (2005) in her research on low levels of information-seeking abilities reported the ironic correlation between low information literacy and a self-perception of higher competency. Low-performing students actually believed they were quite competent and thus did not need to elevate their skill levels. She asserted that 'librarians may have an advantage in their ability to reach low-skill students in instances where literacy instruction is required as part of classwork, for they have the opportunity to work with students of all skill levels' (p. 160). Eisenberg (2006), noting that many secondary school librarians lack status and support, called for librarians to take action regardless. He proposed focusing on three areas: information literacy instruction, reading advocacy, and information management. 'First and foremost', wrote Eisenberg, 'the school librarian is a teacher – primarily of information literacy' (p. 22). Comparing student information literacy skills between schools at different achievement levels under the Mississippi Accountability System is the purpose of the project proposed in this paper.

Assessment studies

While information literacy as a learning component had been well-defined by the year 2000, methods of assessment were lacking. *Information Power: Building Partnerships for Learning*, while covering standards very extensively, had only a brief coverage of assessment strategies, and the few examples given focused mainly on the mechanics of information access by the student rather than an evaluation of quality or achievement. It did, however, provide a general discussion of the assessment process and assessment strategies (pp. 175–81). Pausch and Popp had earlier found that evaluation and assessment were most likely to be informal, and when formal assessment was being done, it was frequently incomplete. Often, formal assessments focused on a single part of a program, such as content, methodology, or effect on student attitudes. They declared that while many institutions have begun teaching information literacy concepts instead of tools, 'few programs have adopted methods aimed at assessing whether students gained the cognitive skills for analysis, synthesis, and evaluation of information that form the basis for much of the assessment of higher education' (1997). The studies also typically lacked any control groups.

Lisa O'Connor, Carolyn Radcliff, and Julie Gedeon sought to address this assessment deficit at the higher education level (2001, online). Their research focused on evaluating two areas: information literacy skills and methods of teaching those skills. They sought to measure information literacy by devising a standardized tool for use in universities. Using standards developed by the American Association of School Libraries and the Association of College and Research Libraries, they identified skills associated with understanding of each standard, then devised easily understandable methods of measuring those skills based on knowledge items of increasing difficulty. The paper cited in this project covered only the early stages of the development of the first instrument. Bonnie Gratch Lindauer presented 'a view of three arenas critical to information literacy learning and assessment, along with questions that might serve as a checklist to stimulate assessment planning and practice' (2004: 122–9). She defined these as the learning environment (curriculum and external learning opportunities), the information literacy program components (courses, workshops, interaction with librarians, and informal independent learning), and student learning outcomes (performance measurements, portfolios, course grades, student self-assessment, and surveys). Lindauer's study was much more comprehensive than the assessment activity proposed in this paper, which would correspond approximately to parts of her information literacy and student learning outcomes arenas.

Cooney and Hiris detailed an assessment process at the C.W. Post campus of Long Island University (2003). It was part of an effort to 'enhance the level of collaboration' (p. 217) between the Center for Business Research and classes in the Graduate School of Business, and used two assessment tools. The first was an IL inventory used as a pre-test to 'briefly assess the students' information-seeking skills and behavior' (p. 219); the second was a more comprehensive outcomes checklist used to evaluate information literacy at the completion of a term project. This assessment evaluation, used at the graduate degree level, shows the importance of information literacy across the educational spectrum. Jennifer Nutefall described the use of an 'annotated portfolio of the research process' (2004: 93) used in a semester-long college course on information literacy. The course was developed specifically to teach and measure information literacy, using six defined assignments and a paper trail which would follow and document the process of satisfying each assignment. Because it involved essentially an ongoing journal of research activities with defined activities and benchmarks throughout the semester, such a process is beyond the scope of this project.

Online assessment studies

Attempts to measure information literacy using online methods are a very recent development. Cameron and Feind (2001) wrote about the use of such a test at James Madison University, which evolved from a paper-based assessment developed in 1998. They noted that '(S)tudents may come in as individuals and take the test, or General Education faculty may schedule whole classes to take the test at once' (p. 214). The online test at James Madison University is designed specifically for the university, which includes information literacy as part of the General Education curriculum and includes the student's score on this test as part of their student record. O'Connor, Radcliff, and Gedeon (2002) reported on their project to 'develop an instrument for programmatic-level assessment of information literacy skills that is valid – and thus credible – to university administrators and other academic personnel' (p. 528). They wanted a standardized assessment vehicle that could be used by many universities and colleges and failed to find an existing example.

The product of their efforts, not completed at the time of their 2002 paper, was an instrument called Project SAILS (Project for the Standardized Assessment of Information Literacy Skills). Begun as a pen-and-paper evaluative tool for assessment of 'the information literacy skills of students longitudinally and across institutions' (p. 529), it was changed during the development process to a web-based format, which the authors noted offered:

> advantages over paper, primarily in terms of data collection. Web responses going directly into a database cut out the tedious and

expensive step of data entry and substantially reduce the potential for errors. It also is possible to work with instructors to have students complete the questionnaire outside class time without the additional time and staffing demands of getting the proper forms to the students, collecting the completed responses, and meeting other administrative challenges. (p. 541)

Correspondence with the authors of this project led to the identification of TRAILS as a potential instrument for the research proposed in this paper. Lisa O'Connor and Julie Gedeon were associated with the development team for both projects. TRAILS is a web-based tool for 'knowledge assessment with multiple-choice questions targeting a variety of information literacy skills appropriate for high-school students ... developed to provide an easily accessible and flexible tool for library media specialists and teachers to identify strengths and weaknesses in the information-seeking skills of their students' (online, *http://www.trails9.org/*).

Methodology

The TRAILS assessments were scrutinized for correlation with AASL standards. Most of the Standards set forth by the AASL dealing with the ability to locate and evaluate information are assessed in this instrument. AASL Standards not tested are those dealing with the students' appreciation of literature and creative expression and how the student contributes information to the learning community – sharing and collaborating with others. Since AASL provides the information literacy objectives for the State of Mississippi, it was determined that this was an appropriate instrument to evaluate the information literacy skills of high-school students late in the 11th grade. The TRAILS instrument assessed five broad categories:

1. *Developing the topic* – developing focus; recognizing the hierarchical relationships of broader and narrower topics; identifying individuals to help focus a topic; and identifying manageable topics.

2. *Identifying potential sources* – understanding where information is located and the types of information available at those locations; finding proper tools; and selecting the most productive sources and tools.

3. *Developing, using, and revising search strategies* – understanding how to use information containers to retrieve information; selecting search terms; developing search strategies; understanding Boolean operators; and revising search strategies when too much or too little information is returned.

4. *Evaluating sources and information* – recognizing bias; differentiating fact and opinion; and determining the accuracy, authority, coverage, currency, and relevancy of information and/or information sources.

5. *Recognizing how to use information responsibly, ethically, and legally* – understanding how to paraphrase correctly; understanding the concepts of intellectual property and intellectual freedom; and creating bibliographies and parenthetical citations according to an appropriate style manual.

(Online, TRAILS, http://www.trails9.org/)

A list of high-school principals was obtained from the Mississippi Department of Education, which included physical addresses, phone numbers, and e-mail addresses for each principal. An e-mail message was sent to each principal inviting their school to participate in this study. In addition, copies of the invitations were posted to the Mississippi Librarian list-serve and the Mississippi Science Teachers list-serve, requesting members of those lists to encourage participation by their schools.

In April, nine envelopes with the research materials were mailed to high schools that indicated they would participate in this study. Three more were delivered by hand to local high schools.

The assumption was made for this project that computer access would be available in each school since the then Mississippi Governor Ronnie Musgrove mandated in 2001 that every classroom in Mississippi would have a computer connected to the Internet. None of the schools participating in the survey indicated that there was a problem providing students access to the Internet. However, the instrument was not dependent on students taking the assessment in school. Teachers had the option of giving students a code along with the Internet address for the instrument and allowing students to access it from home or from another appropriate location, such as a public library. All of the schools that participated in this study gave the assessment under supervision at school.

There are two TRAILS assessment tools and the developers of the program suggest that one instrument be administered as a pre-test in the fall of the year and the other as a post-test in the spring of the same year, or that the assessment be given in the 9th grade and again in a subsequent grade to measure progress. Since this project was to determine baseline data concerning information literacy from students in different locations in the state of Mississippi the assessment was administered only once for the purposes of this study.

The site coordinators were instructed to select a number of students of regular class size (20–25) identified as college-bound 11th grade students, obtain student and parental permissions, set up a session on the TRAILS site, assign each student a number generated by the TRAILS program and keep a record of the numbers and corresponding student names for their records. A copy of the student code numbers with students identified only by race and gender was returned to the project coordinator. Eleventh graders were selected for this study because they should have the information literacy skills being assessed by the instrument used. Practically, however, any information literacy gaps detected in this study would allow the high school another year to correct the deficiency. Since this project was administered in the spring, 10th graders were not chosen for this study because they strictly focus on the state Subject Area Test in English and because they may not have practiced all of the skills measured by this instrument. Students typically complete their first full research paper in the 11th grade and so junior level students should have practiced the skills measured by the TRAILS instrument.

After students finished answering the 30 items in the assessment, the teacher was asked to close the session, print the student and class reports, keep a copy for their records if they desired, and mail the reports, the class list, and permission forms to the project coordinator. Also completed and mailed to the coordinator was a brief questionnaire of general information about the school which was included in the introductory letter. After receiving all student surveys, the results were scrutinized by mean class score and by categories of responses. Patterns were analyzed and scores of level 4 (advanced) and 5 (excellent) schools were compared to those of level 3 (successful) schools to determine discrepancies in information literacy skills. No schools of levels 2 (warned) or 1 (probation) participated in the assessment.

Results

Multiple e-mails were sent to 231 high schools in Mississippi extending an invitation to take part in this research project and explaining the benefits of participation. Fifteen schools responded and indicated that they would administer the survey. Nine packets were sent by mail to those schools, and three were hand-delivered to schools in close vicinity to the research coordinator. Of the 15 schools that indicated via e-mail that they would participate in this information literacy survey, five schools returned a completed survey.

Designated site coordinators in five high schools in Mississippi, ranging in state accreditation levels from 3 to 5, selected 11th-grade college-bound students to represent their school in an information literacy survey conducted April/May 2007.

Site coordinators of this survey were allowed to choose the students they wished to represent the school. Social studies teachers were selected at the level 5 schools as site coordinators. One social studies teacher (School 4) used her Advanced Placement class as test subjects, the other asked for volunteers from students passing in the hall. It is apparent by examining the score range and the standard deviation score which group was the random sample and which was the grouped selection. The range and standard deviation was much less in the Advanced Placement class and the mean score was higher than in the randomly selected group. There was no specific information given on how subjects were selected by the remaining site coordinators, two of whom were librarians and one of whom was an 11th-grade English teacher.

All teachers reported the instrument easy to set up and use. The only complaint reported was an inability to delete students from the total number once the class list was set up. This problem was reported by the teacher to the project director of TRAILS and to the director of this survey. It did not affect the survey results. There were no problems reported concerning student difficulties using the instrument. In fact, one teacher reported that the students enjoyed taking the survey.

Quantitative analysis

Tables A2.1 to A2.5 show the number and percentage of correct answers for each school and for each question within categories (note that some questions had more than one correct answer). 'Each single-correct-response item (question) is worth one point. Each response of a multiple-correct-response item is worth one point, because not checking a wrong (distractor) response is worth as much as checking a correct response. E.g., a score of zero to five is possible from a five-response, multiple-correct-response item' (from the Class Report generated by TRAILS, *www.trails9.org/*).

Table A2.1 Developing topics – number and percentage of correct responses

High school	Level	Q1			Q2	Q3	Q4	Q5
		A	C	D	C	A	C	A
HS 1	3	16 (100%)	6 (38%)	7 (44%)	4 (25%)	10 (63%)	5 (31%)	12 (75%)
HS 2	3	14 (82%)	9 (53%)	7 (41%)	6 (35%)	8 (47%)	6 (35%)	8 (47%)
HS 3	4	22 (88%)	12 (48%)	11 (44%)	11 (44%)	15 (60%)	13 (52%)	17 (68%)
HS 4	5	9 (82%)	7 (64%)	4 (36%)	7 (64%)	10 (91%)	5 (46%)	10 (91%)
HS 5	5	22 (92%)	10 (42%)	8 (33%)	11 (46%)	15 (63%)	10 (42%)	17 (71%)

Question 1 asked which individual could help a student focus their topic. The first correct response was their teacher, and subsequent correct answers were the school librarian and public librarian. It is perhaps telling that fewer than half of the respondents thought that librarians could help focus their topic. Questions 2 through 5 dealt with determining whether a topic was too narrow or too broad, and other than high-school (HS) 4, which used advanced placement students for their survey group, the results show that topic development is a weakness.

Table A2.2 Identifying sources – number and percentage of correct responses

High school	Level	Q6	Q7	Q8	Q9	Q10	Q11
		C	C	A	B	E	B
HS 1	3	7 (44%)	5 (31%)	11 (69%)	16 (100%)	16 (100%)	16 (100%)
HS 2	3	10 (59%)	8 (47%)	8 (47%)	15 (88%)	13 (77%)	15 (88%)
HS 3	4	13 (52%)	9 (36%)	19 (76%)	25 (100%)	24 (96%)	25 (100%)
HS 4	5	1 (9%)	5 (46%)	10 (91%)	11 (100%)	10 (91%)	11 (100%)
HS 5	5	14 (58%)	10 (42%)	11 (46%)	24 (100%)	20 (83%)	22 (92%)

Question 6, on identifying a current article on steroid use in baseball, showed somewhat similar results for all schools except for the HS 4 advanced placement students. The unexpectedly low score of the advanced placement students in HS 4 may be a case of the respondents 'thinking too hard', focusing on the science aspect of steroid use rather than general newsworthiness. Questions 7 through 11 all tended to be clustered fairly close to the mean, with the exception of question 8, dealing with the terms primary source, secondary source, and tertiary source. Again, the advanced placement students from HS 4 were the outliers, perhaps indicating students more familiar with research terminology due to additional class research assignments.

Question 12 required some basic familiarity with MLA-style citations, and other than the group of advanced placement students, the results were relatively poor. Questions 13 and 18 asked about Boolean operators, and the low percentages for most schools indicate a need for basic instruction in Boolean operations. Question 14 asked which type of online search would be appropriate for the given information, and while on the surface it would appear that three groups did very well on this particular question – the search phrase was the title of a very popular book (*Harry Potter and the Sorcerer's Stone*) – it is possible that the percentage of correct answers has more to do with familiarity with that particular book rather than familiarity with online search tools. Question 15 asked the students to order the steps of a research project, and in each school roughly half of the students answered correctly. Each school performed best on question 16, which asked which part of a book would tell you what chapters were in the book. Poorest results for all schools except one came from question 18, which required testers to identify the correct Boolean operator for a specific situation.

Questions 19, 21, and 22 required the respondents to assess a source or piece of information, while questions 20, 23, and 24 concerned definitions. Again, other than the HS 4 advanced placement students, the responses indicate weak evaluative skills. For most schools, the best results came from question 21, although one school which did poorly on that question performed best of all schools on question 22. The worst performance for most schools was on question 24; the advanced placement students did relatively well on that question, but had the poorest results of all schools on question 23.

Questions 25 and 26 required respondents to be able to understand MLA-style citations, and unlike question 12, which also dealt with a citation, most students did well. Questions 27, 28, and 29 were concept definitions, and most students answered correctly, except on question 28, where they seemed to lack understanding of the differences between fair use, freedom of information, intellectual freedom, and intellectual property. Question 30 asked about the legality of using images on the Web, and well over half of the students knew that the owner of an image must give permission for it to be used on a website. Given the proliferation of copied pictures and other media among teenaged users

Table A2.3 Develop and use search strategies – number and percentage of correct answers

High school	Level	Q12	Q13			Q14	Q15	Q16	Q17	Q18
		A	A	B	C	C	C	D	B	E
HS 1	3	11 (69%)	10 (63%)	9 (57%)	11 (69%)	10 (63%)	8 (50%)	14 (88%)	9 (56%)	4 (25%)
HS 2	3	4 (23%)	7 (41%)	6 (35%)	11 (64%)	9 (53%)	7 (41%)	16 (94%)	8 (47%)	3 (18%)
HS 3	4	17 (68%)	19 (76%)	21 (84%)	14 (56%)	24 (96%)	11 (44%)	24 (96%)	17 (68%)	7 (28%)
HS 4	5	10 (91%)	7 (64%)	5 (46%)	5 (46%)	10 (91%)	6 (55%)	11 (100%)	5 (46%)	3 (27%)
HS 5	5	13 (54%)	15 (63%)	14 (59%)	6 (25%)	22 (92%)	14 (58%)	23 (96%)	17 (71%)	7 (29%)

Table A2.4 Evaluate sources and information – number and percentage of correct answers

High school	Level	Q19	Q20	Q21			Q22	Q23	Q24
		C	B	A2	B3	C3	E	D	E
HS 1	3	7 (44%)	8 (50%)	10 (63%)	8 (50%)	3 (19%)	13 (81%)	11 (69%)	1 (6%)
HS 2	3	3 (18%)	10 (59%)	13 (77%)	6 (35%)	11 (65%)	11 (65%)	7 (41%)	2 (12%)
HS 3	4	11 (44%)	12 (48%)	19 (76%)	17 (68%)	11 (44%)	10 (40%)	11 (44%)	7 (28%)
HS 4	5	8 (73%)	9 (82%)	10 (91%)	10 (91%)	9 (82%)	8 (73%)	3 (27%)	7 (64%)
HS 5	5	11 (46%)	14 (58%)	14 (58%)	11 (46%)	11 (46%)	11 (46%)	9 (38%)	9 (38%)

Table A2.5 Using information responsibly, ethically, and legally – number and percentage of correct responses

High school	Level	Q25	Q26	Q27	Q28	Q29	Q30
		D	C	A	B	C	A
HS 1	3	15 (94%)	16 (100%)	12 (75%)	6 (38%)	14 (88%)	8 (50%)
HS 2	3	10 (59%)	15 (88%)	9 (53%)	5 (29%)	17 (100%)	9 (53%)
HS 3	4	20 (80%)	25 (100%)	25 (100%)	13 (52%)	24 (96%)	20 (80%)
HS 4	5	11 (100%)	11 (100%)	11 (100%)	6 (55%)	11 (100%)	9 (82%)
HS 5	5	19 (79%)	20 (83%)	19 (79%)	12 (50%)	20 (83%)	15 (63%)

of the Internet, it is interesting to note that 64 percent or more in each school responded either correctly, or that it was not legal to use the image at all.

Table A2.6 shows the average percentage of correct answers on questions within the five categories assessed by the TRAILS instrument. Only correct answers are shown.

With the small number of responses, it is not possible to make many definitive statements. It is apparent, however, that while Mississippi 11th-graders have some knowledge of information literacy, there is room for improvement. Overall, the students performed best in identifying sources and using information responsibly. Poorest performance was in the areas of developing topics, developing and using search strategies, and evaluating sources. No single school stood out, although the level 5 school which used AP history students as testers (high school 4) had the

Table A2.6 Average percent correct by category

School and number of students	Level	Developing topics	Identifying sources	Developing and using search strategies	Evaluating sources	Using information responsibly
High School 1 (16)	3	53.6	74.0	59.7	47.7	74.0
High School 2 (21)	3	48.8	67.7	46.4	46.3	63.7
High School 3 (25)	4	57.7	76.7	68.4	49.0	84.7
High School 4 (11)	5	67.5	72.7	62.6	72.7	89.4
High School 5 (24)	5	55.4	70.1	60.6	46.9	72.9

highest scores in three of the five categories. The level 4 school (high school 3) had the highest scores in the other two categories.

Table A2.7 compares range, mean, and standard deviation scores of schools of different accreditation levels. Maximum score is 38. Total number of students assessed was 97.

Table A2.7 Range, mean, and standard deviation scores by school

	Number of students assessed	School accreditation level	Range of scores	Mean	Std dev.
School 1	16	3	19–28	24	3
School 2	21	3	9–29	21	5.39
School 3	25	4	16–32	26	4.09
School 4	11	5	23–33	27.64	2.5
School 5	24	5	8–35	23.13	7.08

Additional information collected from schools is reported in Table A2.8. The additional information revealed that all schools had a library and all except school 1, which reported nothing, indicated that students had a minimum of 37 hours of school library service provided per week. All libraries were staffed with one certified librarian except school 1

Table A2.8 Additional information

School	Accred. level	School size	Certified librarian	Add. staff	Library hrs per day	Computers	Books per student	Community	Geography
1	3	500–1,000	0	1		25	14	Rural	Northwest MS
2	3	0–500	1	0	37	8	10	Rural	Central MS
3	4	1,000+	1	1	40+	7	7.86	Rural	Northeast MS
4	5	1,000+	1	1	40+	13	12	Suburban	Central MS
5	5	1,000+	1	1	40+	16	8	Suburban	Central MS

which had a library assistant (paraprofessional) in charge of the library. Every school reported having multiple computers with Internet accessibility available for student use. Number of books available for student use ranged from 7.86 to 14 books per student. Three of the schools that participated in the research project were rural and two were suburban.

Discussion

The Presidential Committee on Information Literacy determined in 1989 that information literacy skills were absolutely necessary in our current society for people to participate effectively in business and the democratic way of life. Schools were charged with promoting equality for all citizens by creating programs that taught young people how to seek out appropriate information, to evaluate sources for bias and authenticity, and to effectively use and communicate data. Almost a decade later, in 1998, the Update on the ALA Presidential Committee on Information Literacy: Final Report stated emphatically that 'State Departments of Education, Commissions on Higher Education and Academic Governing Boards should be responsible to ensure that a climate conducive to students becoming information literate exists in their states and on their campuses' (ALA, 1989: 8). It is clear that information literacy has been determined to be the great leveler among all types of people and should be a priority in institutions charged with education. The ability to locate, evaluate, and utilize information is necessary not only to write effective research papers for secondary and higher education, but to run businesses successfully and to enhance our daily lives in a multitude of ways.

The current newsletter distributed by the Mississippi Department of Education (MDE) headlines an article on 'Redesigning Education for the 21st Century Workforce – A Plan for Mississippi' which declares 'Mississippi high school graduates will be prepared academically as well as equipped with learning and thinking skills, global awareness, information and communications technology literacy and life skills' (cover page, *MDE Brief*, 2006). This issue of the *MDE Brief* proclaims the thrust toward information and communications technology literacy should be a main concern for Mississippi educators. Information and Media Literacy is listed in the 7th, 8th, and 9th grade standards as an instructional component. Plainly, the Superintendent of Education in Mississippi and his advisors understand the need for information literacy skills as they are a stated part of this important agenda.

How can educators say they are satisfying this essential objective if they do not measure student information literacy? Bonnie Gratch Lindauer in her article 'The Three Arenas of Information Literacy Assessment' suggests that lack of expertise, lack of time, and lack of financial and/or human resources may be some of the reasons why measurement of information literacy skills might not be done. The TRAILS information literacy survey breaks down all of these barriers to measuring these abilities. The instrument is online, quick, user friendly, free of charge, and created and maintained by experts in this field. In addition, it provides quantitative data for educators and administrators making it easy to identify deficiencies in student proficiencies within the categories evaluated by the survey.

The purpose of this project was to evaluate the information literacy skills of a sample of students in Mississippi in schools of varying accreditation levels to see if schools and educators are successfully imparting these skills to their charges. The TRAILS instrument was chosen as the tool to accomplish this purpose.

The TRAILS instrument was designed primarily to evaluate the general literacy standards set forth by the AASL which are the standards used in Mississippi. The instrument measures skills in five major categories: Developing Topic, Identifying Potential Sources, Developing, Using, and Revising Search Strategies, Evaluating Sources and Information and Recognizing How to Use Information Responsibly, Ethically, and Legally. The survey is intended to be given initially to students at grade level 9. Students, by the end of grade 11, should have mastered the skills assessed in this instrument if the stated standards have been met. In the spring of 2007 five public schools ranging in accreditation levels 3–5 selected 11th grade, college-bound students to take this survey. The results were sent to the research project coordinator to be evaluated.

Analysis of data

The overall average percentages in Table A2.2 show that the surveyed students were fairly proficient in identifying sources and knowing how to use information responsibly and ethically. They were less capable at evaluating sources, and were similarly weak at developing topics and developing search strategies. Even the known advanced placement students performed poorly on those three categories.

When the respondents were asked questions about topic development, they tended to answer correctly when they were asked to determine whether a revised topic was broader or narrower than the original topic. They did not perform as well when the question was less specific, determining whether a suggested topic was too broad, too narrow, or appropriate. They performed worst when asked to decide the broadest topic within a group of related concepts. Their responses showed they did not view school or public librarians as being helpful in focusing a topic.

While identifying potential sources was one of the better overall categories, examination of the individual questions paints a somewhat different picture. The students did very well when asked where they could best get help with library research or where to find a new book. But when asked to identify a potential source for a topic, they performed far worse.

Developing search strategies was another weak category for students at all schools, and the scores would have been even worse if not for one question about a Harry Potter novel. In particular, the results argue for increased instruction about Boolean operations and concepts such as keywords, both of which are essential for any but the simplest searches.

Overall, the worst performance was on evaluating sources, and the lowest percentages of correct answers came on questions which asked about definitions of terms including coverage, currency, and authority. Only the advanced placement students at high school 4 showed a familiarity with the terms.

The strongest category for most schools was using information responsibly, legally, and ethically. In contrast to the other categories, students displayed a firm grasp of the surveyed concepts. With the exception of one question which asked them to identify the correct concept from a list including fair use, freedom of information, intellectual freedom, intellectual property, and right to privacy, most schools had 80 percent or more correct answers on all questions. Whether from formal instruction or awareness of current societal issues, most students showed an understanding of copyright and plagiarism issues.

Additional information collected from schools revealed that all schools had a library and all except school 1, which reported nothing, indicated that students had a minimum of 37 hours of school library service provided per week. All libraries were staffed with one certified librarian except school 1 which had a paraprofessional in charge of the library. Every school reported having multiple computers with Internet accessibility available for student use. Number of books available for student use ranged from 7.86 to 14 books per student. Three of the schools that participated in the research project were rural and two were suburban. All schools show evidence of having the facilities and tools available to ensure students develop information literacy skills. An added benefit of this survey was that of making principals, teachers, and librarians across the state aware of this newly developed, free instrument for assessing information literacy skills.

Suggestions for the future

1. This pilot study suggests that students in Mississippi are not adequately versed in information literacy skills identified by the state. Further evaluation with greater numbers should be done using the TRAILS information literacy assessment.

2. For future testing, site coordinators should be selected on a more uniform basis – i.e. all 11th grade regular English teachers.

3. For testing in the future, students within schools should be selected more uniformly using a specified method in order to compare groups more accurately. Groups of students may be heterogeneously or homogeneously selected.

4. Principals and teachers in Mississippi in all academic areas should receive inservice training on the importance of information literacy skills for students and how information literacy applies to all academic areas. They should be educated in current methods of locating, evaluating, and utilizing information.

5. English teachers and librarians in Mississippi should be trained in the use of the TRAILS information literacy assessments.

6. The TRAILS information literacy assessments should be used at several points during a student's high-school years to evaluate progress at the beginning and end of a particular grade or progress between grade levels.

Conclusion

With the small number of student responses available in this study, it is not possible to make many definitive statements regarding the information literacy of Mississippi students. It is apparent, however, that while Mississippi 11th-graders have some knowledge of information literacy, there is considerable room for improvement.

The first investigative question of this study was: 'How well do the 11th grade students in this study perform on the TRAILS Information

Literacy Quiz?' The results of this study were somewhat disappointing. The TRAILS assessment survey is based on the same information literacy standards used in the state of Mississippi and while students in Mississippi showed proficiency in some areas of information literacy, they did not demonstrate mastery of all or even most of the basic skills the state standards mandate. By the end of the 11th grade most students should demonstrate such a competence. Most students performed well in the areas of identifying sources and using information responsibly, legally, and ethically. Students demonstrated a lack of knowledge in the areas of developing search strategies, evaluating sources, and developing topics.

The second research question was: 'If students lack literacy skills, in what skills are they deficient?' One of the most obvious areas is Boolean search operators and techniques. Barely half of the students correctly answered one question concerning Boolean operators, while only a quarter correctly answered a second question. This finding is similar to the research done by Cameron and Feind at James Madison University, where they noted that questions about using Boolean operators were among the most often missed on their assessment instrument (2001: 217). The tested students also performed poorly on questions which asked them to assess whether a given topic was too narrow or too broad. The students in the Mississippi survey also displayed problems with search strategies and evaluating potential sources. Again, this is echoed by the results of the James Madison University study, which found that, in addition to difficulties with Boolean operators, the most often missed questions concerned development of effective search strategies, locating journal articles, and understanding keyword and subject searches (2001: 217). Cameron and Feind also found that students generally had a clear understanding of information ethics, which was also shown by the survey of Mississippi high-school students. The generally poor performance of student testers in this assessment on questions about evaluation of sources is given emphasis by Levine's research concerning online misinformation and the role of schools in overcoming this problem (2005).

The third research question asked was: 'Do students in schools with lower accreditation ratings lack literacy skills possessed by students in higher-rated schools?' The data gathered by this study compared schools with a level 3 accreditation rating to schools with levels 4 and 5 accreditation ratings. Overall, the mean score of students in the schools with lower accreditation levels was comparable to those in schools given higher accreditation levels. All schools reported having tools that help students develop literacy skills, well-equipped libraries, an adequate number of library hours, and, with the exception of high school 1 (a level 3 school), a certified librarian.

The results of this study indicate that students participating in the assessment understand that there are responsible, ethical, and legal ways to use information. They do not, however, have a clear understanding of concepts such as fair use, freedom of information, and intellectual property. They are generally able to identify types of sources of information – books or magazines, encyclopedias, or online databases. But they are not adept at searching for specific sources of information, and evaluating those sources once they have been found. As shown in Table A2.6, other than the advanced placement students, the results for all categories are consistent across accreditation levels. Little differentiation was noted between suburban and rural areas, or between different geographical areas of the state, or between schools of different size.

This is a pilot study and as such should not be viewed as a comprehensive assessment of information literacy among Mississippi high-school students. The results do have value as indicators of a potential weakness of certain information literacy skills across all accreditation levels, however, and may be used to develop more focused information literacy teaching materials. A more complete finding would require the participation of more schools and students. It is recommended that this study be expanded to include a greater number of schools, representing each accreditation level of the Mississippi Department of Education and drawn from each geographical region of the state.

References cited

American Association of School Libraries and the Association for Educational Communications and Technology (1998) *Information Power: Building Partnerships for Learning.* Chicago: American Library Association.

American Library Association (1989) *Presidential Committee on Information Literacy: Final Report.* Chicago: American Library Association.

American Library Association (1998) *A Progress Report on Information Literacy: An Update on the American Library Association Presidential Committee on Information Literacy: Final Report.* Chicago: American Library Association.

Association of College and Research Libraries (2000) *Information Literacy Competency Standards for Higher Education.* Chicago: Association of College and Research Libraries.

Banta, T.W., Lund, J.P., Black, K.E., and Oblander, F.W. (1996) *Assessment in Practice: Putting Principles to Work on College Campuses.* San Francisco: Jossey-Bass.

Big6: Information skills for student achievement. Online at: *http://www.big6.com.*

Cameron, L. and Feind, R. (2001) 'An online competency test for information literacy: development, implementation, and results.' Retrieved August 23, 2006 from: *http://www.ala.org/ala/acrl/acrlevents/cameron.pdf.*

Cooney, M. and Hiris, L. (2003) 'Integrating information literacy and its assessment into a graduate business course: a collaborative framework,' *Research Strategies*, 19(3/4): 213–32.

Darrow, R. and MacDonald, C. (2004) 'What is information literacy in the digital age?' *CSLA Journal*, 27(2): 21–3.

Eisenberg, M. (2006) 'Three roles for the 21st-century teacher-librarian,' *CSLA Journal*, 29(2): 21–3.

Ercegovac, Z. (2003) 'Bridging the knowledge gap between secondary and higher education,' *College & Research Libraries*, 64(1): 75–85.

Gross, M. (2005) 'The impact of low-level skills on information-seeking behavior,' *Reference & User Services Quarterly*, 45(2): 155–62.

Leu, D. and Kinzer, C. (2000) 'The convergence of literacy instruction with networked technologies for information and communication,' *Reading Research Quarterly*, 35(1): 108–27.

Levine, P. (2005) 'The problem of online misinformation and the role of schools,' *Studies in Media & Information Literacy Education*, 5(1).

Lindauer, B., Arp, L., and Woodard, B. (2004) 'The three arenas of information literacy assessment,' *Reference & User Services Quarterly*, 44(2): 122–9. Retrieved March 22, 2006, from Academic Search Premier.

Mackey, T. and Ho, J. (2005) 'Implementing a convergent model for information literacy: combining research and web literacy,' *Journal of Information Science*, 31(6): 541–55.

Mississippi School Library Media Guide (2002) Mississippi Department of Education, pp. 18–20. Retrieved March 20, 2007 from: *http://www.mde.k12.ms.us/ACAD/ID/Curriculum/Library/librarymedia_guide.doc.*

Nutefall, J. (2004) 'Paper trail: one method of information literacy assessment,' *Research Strategies*, 20(1/2): 89–98.

O'Connor, L., Radcliff, C., and Gedeon, J. (2001) 'Assessing information literacy skills: developing a standardized instrument for institutional and longitudinal measurement,' in *Crossing the Divide: Proceedings of the Tenth National Conference of the Association of College and*

Research Libraries. Chicago: ACRL. Retrieved April 16, 2006 from: *http://www.ala.org/ala/acrl/acrlevents/oconnor.pdf*.

O'Connor, L., Radcliff, C., and Gedeon, J. (2002) 'Applying systems design and item response theory to the problem of measuring information literacy skills,' *College & Research Libraries*, 63(6): 528.

Owusu-Ansah, E. (2003) 'Information literacy and the academic library: a critical look at a concept and the controversies surrounding it,' *Journal of Academic Librarianship*, 29(4): 219–30.

Pausch, L. and Popp, M. (1997) *Assessment of Information Literacy: Lessons from the Higher Education Assessment Movement*, ACRL 1997 national conference papers. Chicago: Association of College and Research Libraries. Retrieved April 24, 2006 from: *http://www.ala .org/ala/acrlbucket/nashville1997pap/pauschpopp.htm*.

Ratteray, O. (2002) 'Information literacy in self-study and accreditation,' *Journal of Academic Librarianship*, 28(6): 368–75.

'Redesigning Education for the 21st Century Workforce' (2006) *MDE Brief*, 1(1): 1–5.

Smalley, T. (2004) 'College success: high school librarians make the difference,' *Journal of Academic Librarianship*, 30(3): 193–8.

Street, C. (2005) 'Tech talk for social studies teachers,' *Social Studies*, 96(6): 271–3.

TRAILS Assessment. Online at: *http://www.trails9.org/*.

Appendix 3
An Examination of the Scholarly Literature Related to School Libraries and Their Impact on Student Achievement

Glenda Ford, University of Southern Mississippi, December 1, 2009

Introduction

This is the Information Age and information literacy is a fundamental component in the education of children who must be equipped to evaluate information competently. This evaluation includes accessing and using information in both electronic and print forms.

School libraries and credentialed school librarians play a fundamental role in promoting information literacy and reading for information and inspiration. By collaborating with teachers and engaged students, librarians connect them with meaningful information that matters in the twenty-first-century world. This connection can lead to opportunities for achievement for all regardless of socio-economic or education levels in the community.

Budget cuts are having an impact on school libraries all over the United States. Even affluent neighborhoods with schools that have outstanding programs and students with high test scores are contemplating cuts. In some areas retiring media specialists are not being replaced and department directors for library services are facing elimination. There is not one particular state or area in which this is occurring. From Connecticut to California and places in between, cuts are occurring to library positions:

- The California state superintendent of public instruction, Jack O'Connell, recently announced that 20,000 teachers, librarians, counselors, nurses, and support staff were being cut for the upcoming school year. These measures were brought about because of the state's deficit and proposed $4.8 billion education cut (*School Library Journal*, 2008).

- In Westport, Connecticut, high schools with high test scores and a high school that was named 'best' in the state expects first-time cuts that will impact the district's library media program.

- Library media assistants in elementary schools will be cut to half-time (Staino, 2009). Libraries are not the only thing facing budget cuts.

- In Detroit, one principal drew national attention when she asked parents to donate light bulbs and toilet paper to help her school make it through the school year (Billups, 2009).

- Currently Los Angeles' Las Virgines Unified School district has a full-time teacher librarian at each high school, middle school, and elementary school along with a half-time and full-time clerk. The administration and board are now considering cutting all teacher librarians and two tech teachers, and replacing them with three newly created positions. The new positions would emphasize delivering technology to teachers and not working directly with students in libraries. Three people will end up trying to do the work of eight people (Billups, 2009).

To prevent further cuts, librarians need to be armed with facts and information and the public made aware of the contribution that school libraries make to the academic achievement of students. Studies have been made that document such a contribution.

By examining publication and authorship patterns of scholarly literature librarians will be armed with the information needed to inform supervisors, school board members, parents and the general public of the major contributions that the Library Media Specialist (LMS) makes to the local school. For too long librarians and media specialists have not taken a proactive stand. It is time that this information is released and relationships cemented between LMSs, principals, teachers, board members, students and the general public.

Problem statement

The purpose of this study is to examine the publication pattern and authorship of the scholarly literature related to student academic success/achievement and school libraries, including how much has been published on this topic per year, in which journals they were published, and authorship of the articles.

Research questions

RQ1   How many scholarly articles on student academic success/ achievement and school libraries are published per year?
RQ2   In which journals are these articles published?
RQ3   Who authored the articles in this study?
RQ4   Are the authors of the articles in this study school librarians, academic faculty, or other?

Limitations/delimitations

This study includes peer-reviewed, scholarly journal articles but does not include letters to the editor, reviews or opinion columns.

Definitions

Achievement: (1) The act of achieving; (2) a thing achieved, esp. by skill, work, courage, etc. (Neufeldt, 1988).
Bibliometric: The use of statistical methods in the analysis of a body of literature to reveal the historical development of subject fields and patterns of authorship, publication, and use; formerly called statistical bibliography (Mondofacto, n.d.).
Bradford's Law: The bibliometric principle that a disproportionate share of the significant research results on a given subject are published in a relatively small number of the scholarly journals in the field, a pattern of exponentially diminishing returns first noted by Samuel C. Bradford in 1934 (Welsh, 2009).
Collaboration: (1) To work together, esp. in some literary, artistic, or scientific undertaking (Neufeldt, 1988).
Flexible scheduling: Teachers schedule time for their classes to use the library as needed, accompany their class to the library, and collaborate with the library media specialist (American Library Association, 2009).
Information literacy: The ability to recognize when information is needed and have the ability to locate, evaluate, and use effectively the needed information (American Library Association, 2009).

Information power: A standard endorsed by the ALA that outlines a specific plan for school library media specialists and teachers to share the responsibilities of planning, teaching, and assessing student learning and offering a truly cohesive curriculum (American Library Association, 2009).

Library media centers (LMC) or school library media centers: The location in a school where information is available in different formats both print and electronic; materials and activities correspond with classroom activity and students learn information literacy skills (American Library Association, 2009).

Lotka's Law: Lotka's Law of Scientific Productivity is the bibliometric principle that most scholarly authors will contribute only one article to the scholarly literature on a given subject or in a given field (Welsh, 2009).

School library media specialist: The count of professional staff members and supervisors who are assigned specific duties and school time for professional library and media service activities (American Library Association, 2009).

Standards for the 21st-century learner: '... offer vision for teaching and learning to both guide and beckon our profession as education leaders. They will both shape the library program and serve as a tool for library media specialists to use to shape the learning of students in the school' (American Library Association, 2009).

Assumptions

It is assumed that the database articles in this study are indexed accurately and completely so that all pertinent articles are retrieved. Further it is assumed that the items retrieved are representative of the body of work on the subject. It is assumed that author information included with each article is accurate.

Literature review

School library impact studies

During the past two decades a variety of organizations have performed studies 'that cite the measurable impact school libraries and library media specialists have on student achievement' (US NCLIS, 2008: 1).

One such study, *School Libraries Work!*, has recently been updated. Included are excerpts from a Congressional presentation made by the National Commission on Libraries and Information Science in June 2007, and new study results from Delaware, Indiana, Wisconsin and the Canadian province of Ontario. Included in the updated report are new data, statistics, resources, and strategies to help principals, school board members, teachers and library media specialists as they support and improve their library media program.

There is mounting evidence that there is a measurable difference in school achievement where school libraries are staffed by certified library media specialists. Standardized reading achievement scores or global assessments of learning are all measurements of the powerful force that school libraries and library media specialists have in the lives of America's children.

The US NCLIS (National Commission on Libraries and Information Science) Chairman C. Beth Fitzsimmons reported that:

> From our perspective, a critical part of the comprehensive and renewed strategy to ensure that students learn to read and are effective users of information and ideas is the requirement that every school have a school library and that school libraries be staffed by highly qualified, state certified, school library media specialists. (US NCLIS, 2008: 1)

Since 1990 a sizeable body of research has been accumulated that shows a positive relationship between school libraries and student achievement. School libraries can have a positive impact on student achievement whether the achievement is measured by reading scores, literacy, or learning more generally. When a school library is adequately staffed, resourced, and funded it can lead to higher student achievement regardless of the socio-economic or educational levels of the community (US NCLIS, 2008).

Alaska

- Secondary school students with full-time teacher-librarians were almost twice as likely as those without teacher-librarians to score average or above average on the California Achievement Program (CAP).

- Higher test scores came from students who receive library/information literacy instruction from library media specialists.

Colorado

- There was a 21 percent variation in 7th grade Iowa Tests of Basic Skills (ITBS) reading scores, while controlling for socio-economic conditions based on the size of the school library staff and collection.
- Schools that have the most collaborative teacher-librarians in the elementary school level scored 21 percent higher on Colorado Student Assessment Program (CSAP) reading scores than students with the least collaborative teacher-librarians.

Delaware

- School libraries that had state-certified, full-time school librarians, flexible schedules, active instructional programs for information literacy development, and a networked information technology infrastructure helped 98.2 percent of their students in the learning process.
- School libraries that help with reading interest, finding stories, improving reading and helping them enjoy reading more for students in grades 3–5 were credited by the students.
- When school librarians provide individual and class instruction centering on independent information seeking, Internet searching and site evaluation, judging information quality, and interpreting and analyzing information to develop their own ideas, students highly valued the school librarian as a teacher.

Florida

- Library programs in elementary schools staffed 60 hours per week or more have a 9 percent improvement in test scores over those staffed less than 60 hours.
- Library programs staffed 60 hours per week or more have a 3.3 percent improvement in middle schools over those staffed less than 60 hours.
- Library programs of high schools staffed 60 hours per week or more have a 22.2 percent improvement in test scores over those staffed less than 60 hours.

Illinois

- A hallmark of a fully realized school library is one that uses flexible scheduling. Access to strong libraries needs to be as flexible as possible. This enables teachers and students to work with library media specialists and other staff and use the library as a classroom or study space as needed.

- The highest 11th grade ACT scores came from schools where there was a high degree of collaboration between library media specialists and classroom teachers.

Indiana

- An elementary school's library media specialist's tenure is a strong predictor of student proficiency in language arts development. Sixth grade student scores were well above average on the statewide test when the school library media specialist has been with the school full-time for at least three years and excels at both information access and administrative services.
- There seems to be a correlation between higher performing school library media specialists and programs with a supportive administration, collaborative teachers, and an up-to-date resource and technology base.
- Full-time certified library media specialists are more likely to have electronic connections to other school collections and the public library, to secure more federal funding, to provide more frequent instruction in the use of electronic resources, and to maintain a website with links to current and relevant professional resources.

Iowa

- Iowa compared elementary schools with the highest and lowest ITBS reading scores and found the highest scoring students use more than 2½ times as many books and other materials during library visits.
- Reading test scores increase with school library program development. This relationship is not explained away by other school or community conditions at the elementary level.

Massachusetts

- Schools with library programs have higher Massachusetts Comprehensive Assessment System (MCAS) scores at each grade level.

- Elementary and middle/junior high-school-level students score higher on the MCAS test when there is a school library program.

Michigan

- Teachers and students are four times as likely to be able to visit the library on a flexibly scheduled basis in elementary schools with the highest Michigan Educational Assessment Program (MEAP) reading scores, compared to the lowest scoring schools.
- In schools where the library media specialist is certified MEAP reading test scores rise.

Minnesota

- Where the library media specialist worked full-time, the grade 3, 5, and 8 reading tests were above-average in 66.8 percent of the schools.
- Increases in school library program spending are reflected in student reading achievement in elementary and secondary schools.
- Schools with a full-time library media specialist had twice as many above-average scores.

Missouri

- A 10.6 percent statistically significant impact on student achievement was found in schools with library services.
- Missouri Assessment Program (MAP) weighted average index scores rose by 10.6 percent where there were school library services.
- Other school or community demographics did not negate the relationship between school library program services and student achievement.

New Mexico

- Access to licensed databases via a school library network occurred twice as often in New Mexico middle schools with the highest New Mexico Achievement Assessment Program (NMAAP) language arts scores than the lowest scoring schools.
- As the school library program is developed, New Mexico achievement test scores rise.

North Carolina

- Elementary, middle and high schools with school library programs have a significant impact on student achievement as measured by scores on standardized reading and English tests.
- When school libraries have newer books, and were open and staffed more hours during the school week, scores on standardized reading and English tests tended to increase.

Ohio

- Of students in grades 3 to 12, 99.4 percent believe school libraries and their services help them become better learners as reflected in *Student Learning through Ohio School Libraries*.
- Student learning for building knowledge was facilitated by credentialed library media specialists in effective school libraries.

Oregon

- High schools with the best Oregon Statewide Assessment reading/language scores are twice as likely to have teacher–librarian collaboration with classroom teachers as in the lowest scoring schools, and students are three times more likely to visit the library as part of a class or other group.
- School or community conditions at the elementary or middle-school levels or other school conditions at the high-school level are not used to explain away the relationship between school library program development and test scores.
- There seems to be incremental improvements in reading scores in schools where there are incremental improvements in the school's library staffing, collections, and budget.

Pennsylvania

- The promotion of high academic achievement by the school library program depends fundamentally on the presence of adequate staffing – each library should have a minimum of one full-time certified library media specialist along with one full-time aide or support staff member.

- Reading scores on the Pennsylvania System of School Assessment (PSSA) for all three tested grades show a relationship with staffing that is positive and statistically significant.

- In elementary schools with adequate school library staffing there was average or above-average reading scores in 61 percent of the schools, and schools with inadequate library staffing reported below-average scores in the same proportion.

- Middle schools with the best PSSA reading scores spend twice as much on their school libraries as the lowest scoring schools.

- Having a large collection of books, magazines, and newspapers in the school library is not enough to generate high levels of academic achievement by students. These collections have to be a part of a school-wide initiative to integrate information literacy into standards and curriculum.

Texas

- Students in schools with librarians were 10 percent more likely to meet the minimum Texas Assessment of Academic Skills (TAAS) expectations in reading.

- TAAS performance at the elementary, middle/junior high, and high-school levels had an association with library staffing levels, collection sizes, librarian interaction with teachers and students, and library technology levels.

Wisconsin

- The most critical component of the library media program at all school levels is certified library media specialists and aides. Schools with full-time professional librarians or media specialists and support staff have a greater impact on student academic performance.

- Student performance was impacted by library media programs. This impact increased across school levels. At the elementary level the library media program variable was between 3.2 percent and 3.4 percent in reading and language arts performance on state assessment exams; 9.2 percent at the middle-school level; and between 7.9 percent and 19.0 percent at the high-school level.

- School library media programs were more helpful to student performance when teachers aligned the Wisconsin Model Academic Standards for Information and Technology Literacy to their lessons.

- Teaching by library media specialists of information, communication, and technology skills not taught in classrooms but essential for students in the twenty-first century was valued most by students.

- Libraries are the hub of the schools where the best-practice library media programs exist. Library media specialists are highly visible, an integral part of the faculty, and make significant contributions to the curriculum and instructional practices, possessing broad, cross-grade curricular knowledge. They also act as an innovator, transformation agent, and integration technology leader. Teachers consider the library media specialist as an indispensable source of ideas, help, and support. Their expertise is constantly sought.

Ontario, Canada

- The single strongest predictor of reading enjoyment in grades 3 and 6 is the presence of a teacher-librarian.

- Reading enjoyment scores were 8 percentage points higher in schools with teacher-librarians.

- Student achievement and reading enjoyment are linked.

- Reading achievement scores were 5.5 percentage points higher than the average in grade 6 where there were professionally trained school library staff.

- Average achievement and attainment of level 3 or higher was lower in schools without trained library staff.

'Literature of' studies

A 2006 bibliometric study conducted by Patra et al. entitled 'Bibliometric Study of Literature on Bibliometrics' analyzed the growth pattern, core journals, and authors' distribution using data from *Library and Information Science Abstracts (LISA)*. *LISA* is an international abstracting and indexing service designed especially for libraries and information professionals.

The data revealed that there is no definite pattern of literature growth in the field of bibliometrics. *Scientometics* was found to be the core journal with 41 percent of the total literature covered. About 77 percent of authors had only one publication and English was the predominant language. The highest literature growth occurred in 1999 where 208 records were indexed. Over the next few years literature on bibliometrics had a definite growth pattern. This can be attributed to bibliometrics emerging as a new discipline. New subject fields produce huge amounts of literature at the initial stage of their growth. Another contributing factor could have been the advent of computer and information technology (Patra et al., 2006).

Publishing on the topic of bibliometrics occurred primarily in about 280 journals with 3,781 articles. Bradford's Law was used to identify the core journals. Patra reports that this law, better known as Bradford's Law of Scattering, states that 'if scientific journals are arranged in order of decreasing productivity of articles on a given subject, they may be divided into a nucleus of periodicals more particularly devoted to the subject and several other groups or zones containing the same number of articles as the nucleus'. This helps librarians to identify core sets of journals which publish the most in a chosen field. Patra used Lotka's Law that 'is used to find authors, productivity patterns'. According to Lotka's Law of Scientific Productivity, only 6 percent of the authors in a field will produce more than 10 articles (Patra et al., 2006).

Bibliometrics uses unique techniques for the monitoring, evaluation, and analysis of information resources and also for the management of knowledge in social and organizational contents. These methods can be used to analyze the structure of scientific and research areas, and the evolution of research activity and administration of scientific information. Different statistical methods can be used to study authorship, citation and publication pattern, and the relationships within scientific fields and research communities. These types of studies are relevant to researchers, policy and decision-makers, and also researchers outside library and information science. It can help track trends in specific fields of research and help to evaluate research in a particular field in a particular country (Patra et al., 2006).

Another 'literature of' bibliometric study was conducted by Iovino of the University of Southern Mississippi. In the study entitled 'The Civil Rights Movement in Mississippi: A Bibliometric Study in Scholarly Journals,' Iovino studied articles from 1980 to 2000 to determine the growth (or non-growth) of the literature within this particular time period.

Retrieved data showed that there has been a steady increase in the amount published between the years 1980 and 2000. The years 1996 to 2000 showed the greatest increase of 273 percent. A core group of seven journals was found to publish 56.5 percent of the articles. 'Three of the journals are geared toward African American studies, 4 fall under the category of history and 2 have decidedly Southern themes.' The majority of the articles were published in 'journals with historical themes, followed by the African American studies category' (Iovino, 2008). The final categories were Sociology, Education, and Social Studies respectively. Also noted was that authors were not writing about facts tied to events only, but were analyzing and trying to learn from past events in Mississippi's history (Iovino, 2008).

Forty-seven percent of the articles were published in the Northeast, 25.42 percent were published in the Southeast. Two of the core journals were printed in the South with one located in Mississippi. This could be attributed to a reluctance to deal with the subject because of racial tensions that are still in the region or it could be because there are more journals published in the Northeast. No pattern of authorship was shown. Only 18 of the 140 authors were repeat authors. Only three of these have published more than twice on the topic. Most articles were written by a single author. The possibility exists that some of these articles written by some of these authors have been discarded through the years (Iovino, 2008).

The collection analysis showed that the University of Southern Mississippi library system owned 54 of the 59 journals in the study. Not unexpected is the fact that a Mississippi university would have such a strong collection on the Civil Rights movement. Evidence points to a concentrated effort by the university to include as many sources as possible on the subject of Civil Rights in Mississippi (Iovino, 2008).

Methodology

Methodology included an examination of the publication patterns of scholarly literature as it relates to student academic success/achievement and school libraries: how much has been published on this topic per year, the journals that publish the articles, and the authorship of the articles. This information was compiled using Microsoft Excel and Microsoft Word.

The *Library Literature and Information Science* full-text database was searched using the terms 'student achievement' in abstracts and 'librar*' in the abstract field. The limitations of 'full-text' and 'peer-reviewed' were included in the search. In order to extend the list of articles the *EBSCO* database *ERIC* was also added using the same search criteria.

Results

RQ1 How many scholarly articles on student academic success/achievement and school libraries are published per year?

According to the results of this study, 30 articles were published on the impact of school libraries on student achievement from 1998–2009. These findings indicate a peak number of seven articles published during 2005 followed by six articles in 2007. Three articles were published in 2002, 2003, and 2004. Two articles were published in 1999 and 2008; one article was published in 1998, 2001, 2006, and thus far in 2009. No article on this topic was published in 2000. Publication pattern by year is illustrated in Figure A3.1.

Figure A3.1 Number of articles published per year

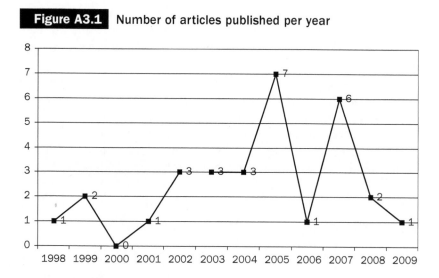

RQ2 In which journals are these articles published?

Upon examination of the sources, it was discovered that *Teacher Librarian* published 60 percent of the articles in this study (see Figure A3.2). *School Libraries Worldwide* published 16 percent of the information. The general principle of Bradford's Law is supported by these findings. It states that a disproportionate share of the scholarly articles on a given subject is published in a relatively small number of the scholarly journals in the field, a pattern of exponentially diminishing returns. Six percent of the articles were published in *Journal of Academic Librarianship*.

Figure A3.2 Core journal titles

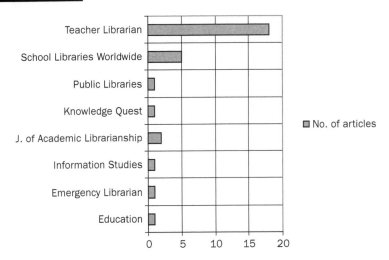

Education, Emergency Librarian, Information Studies, Knowledge Quest, and *School Libraries* each published one peer-reviewed article during the time span of 1998–2009.

RQ3 Who authored the articles in this study?

This research revealed that Haycock authored four of these articles, all appearing in *Teacher Librarian* (see Figure A3.3). Moreillon and Misakian co-authored two articles; the remaining authors wrote only one article each. The general principle of Lotka's Law, which states that

Figure A3.3 Top authors in rank order

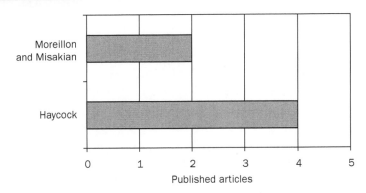

most scholarly authors will contribute only one article to a chosen field or on a given subject, was supported by the results of this research – most of these authors in this study wrote only one article on the subject of the impact of school libraries on student achievement.

RQ4 Are the authors of the articles in this study school librarians, academic faculty, or other?

More than half of the authors teach on a college level, many in the field of library and information science (LIS) (see Figure A3.4). One teaches education at the advanced level. One is an administrator. Professional librarians wrote nine of the articles. The profession of the remaining four is undetermined.

Figure A3.4 Profession of authors

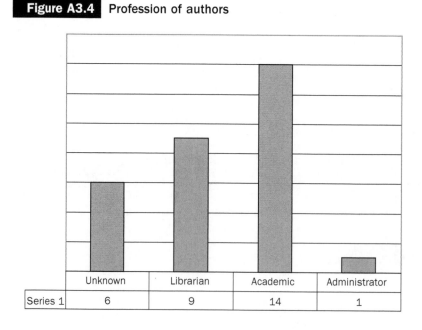

	Unknown	Librarian	Academic	Administrator
Series 1	6	9	14	1

Discussion

Findings indicate that publication of scholarly articles related to the impact that school libraries have on student success seems to have peaked during the year 2005. After 2005, there was a decline in the number of publications per year, followed by a pattern of increasing numbers of publications per year during the past few years, perhaps due to school budget cuts and the need to demonstrate the importance of school libraries to student achievement. Results indicate a 134 percent increase in published articles from 2004 to 2005 in the literature of the impact that school libraries have on student achievement. Another increase of 500 percent was seen in the year from 2006 to 2007.

Data indicate that *Teacher Librarian* and *School Libraries Worldwide* are the two core journals for scholarly articles related to school libraries and their impact on student achievement. Eighteen articles (60 percent) were published in *Teacher Librarian* while *School Libraries Worldwide* published five of the articles (17 percent) in this study. These findings support the general principle of Bradford's Law, which states that a disproportionate share of the scholarly publications on a given subject are published in a relatively small number of the scholarly journals in the field, a pattern of exponentially diminishing returns first noted by Samuel C. Bradford in 1934 (Welsh, 2009).

Haycock may be considered a core author as he is the most prolific author of articles in this study. Haycock published four articles, the most articles published by any single author in this study. The only other authors that published more than one article in this study are Moreillon and Misakian who co-authored two articles published on this topic. The general principle of Lotka's Law, which states that most scholarly authors will contribute only one article to the scholarly literature on a given subject or in a given field (Welsh, 2009), is supported by these findings.

The profession of the three most prolific authors in this study is in the field of academia, which could indicate this topic is in their area of study and research. Nine of the authors reviewed for this study were librarians, one was an administrator, while five of the authors' professions were unknown.

These results indicate the need for further study. As the worldwide economic crisis continues and tax revenues shrink, cuts will probably continue in education spending. For this reason, this study needs to be continued and expanded to include more databases and to extend the time frame of the study.

References

American Library Association, 'AASL School Advocacy Toolkit.' Retrieved on October 19, 2009, from *http://www.ala.org/ala/mgrps/ divs/aasl/aaslissues/toolkits/schoollibrary.cfm*.

American Library Association, 'Final Report from the Presidential Committee on Information Literacy.' Retrieved on October 19, 2009, from: *http://www.ala.org/ala/professionalresources/infolit/index.cfm*.

American Library Association, 'Standards for the 21st Century Learner.' Retrieved on October 19, 2009, from: *http://www.ala.org/ala/mgrps/divs/aasl/guidelinesandstandards/learningstandards/standards.cfm*.

American Library Association and American Association of School Librarians, 'Information Power and Books.' Retrieved on October 19, 2009, from *http://www.ala.org/ala/mgrps/divs/aasl/aaslpubsandjournals/informationpowerbook/informationpowerbooks.cfm*.

American Library Association and American Association of School Librarians, 'School Library Media Specialist's Role in Reading Toolkit.' Retrieved on October 19, 2009, from *http://www.ala.org/ala/mgrps/divs/aasl/aaslissues/toolkits/slmsroleinreading/scenarios.cfm#*.

Billups, A. (2009) 'School budget cuts threaten gains,' *The Washington Times*, March 11, n.p.

Herring, S.D. (2000) 'Journal literature on digital libraries: publishing and indexing patterns, 1992–1997,' *College & Research Libraries*, 1: 39–43.

Iovino, L.A. (2008) 'The Civil Rights Movement in Mississippi: a bibliometric study in scholarly journals,' *Library Student Journal*, 10, n.p.

Mondofacto Ltd (n.d.) *Bibliometric*. Retrieved on October 17, 2009, from: *http://www.mondofacto.com/facts/dictionary?bibliometric*.

Neufeldt, V. (ed.) (1988) *Webster's New World Dictionary of American English*, 3rd edn. New York: Webster's New World.

Patra, S., Bhattacharya, P., and Verma, N. (2006) 'Bibliometric study of literature on bibliometrics,' *Bulletin of Information Technology*, 26: 1.

School Library Journal (2008) 'Pink slips abound: budget cuts take their toll,' April 1, n.p.

Staino, R. (2009) 'Wealthy school libraries feel the pain,' *School Library Journal*, March 9, n.p.

US National Commission on Libraries and Information Science (2008) *School Libraries Work!* Washington, DC. Retrieved October 10, 2009, from: *http://www2.scholastic.com/content/collateral_resources/pdf/s/slw3_2008.pdf*.

Welsh, T. (2009) Bibliometric Laws [class notes]. Retrieved from: *http://www.http://coursites.blackboard.com*.

Appendix 4
A Bibliometric Analysis of Scholarly Literature Related to Information Literacy and Critical Thinking

Linda Matthews, University of Southern Mississippi, December 1, 2009

Knowledge is of two kinds: We know a subject ourselves, or we know where we can find information upon it. (Dr Samuel Johnson, 1709–84)

Introduction

The subject of information literacy is one that has been associated with the field of library and information science for many years. Thirty-five years ago the common term used was 'library skills' and it referred to a finite set of skills a person needed in order to conduct research and find information in a library. With the rise of computers and information systems, library and education professionals recognized that the issue was not just one of accessing the contents of a physical library. Now that Internet-based information has boomed as well, the user must be proficient in tapping into databases, using search engines, and applying Boolean functions as well as using online public access catalogs (OPACs), employing basic computer skills, and navigating through the physical library – and this is just to *find* the information. The bar for information literacy has risen and librarians and educators are now challenged to keep up in providing adequate instruction.

In 1974, Paul Zurchowski first coined the term 'information literacy.' This president of the Information Industry Association described the information literate as those 'people trained in the application of information resources to their work ... They have learned techniques and skills for utilizing the wide range of information tools as well as primary sources in molding information-solutions to their problems.'[1] Through the 1980s and 1990s, this concept was refined, models were built aimed at information literacy education, and a conceptual shift took place that moved the focus from information access to lifelong learning. In 1998, the American Association of School Librarians and the Association for Educational Communications and Technology published *Information Power: Building Partnerships for Learning*. In that document, information literacy (defined as the ability to find and use information) was presented as the keystone of lifelong learning and the school library media specialist was prodded to focus on the process of learning rather than dissemination of information.[2]

What quickly emerged as a core underlying concept to information literacy was 'critical thinking.' The two are tightly connected when it comes to the topic of scholarly inquiry – research. Scholars, particularly students, need not only to find information but to evaluate both the information and its source. This explains why information literacy and critical thinking (as linked skills) form a hot-button issue at institutions of higher learning. Academic libraries have found no single 'correct' approach to instruction in this area and accrediting agencies have handed down less-than-precise standards to be met. However, many colleges and universities have discovered that the best approach seems to be to integrate information literacy instruction into various courses to provide a context for the critical thinking part of the equation. While there is a trend in the literature to suggest that this contextual instruction yields better results than library-centric instruction, little concrete data have been provided to support this contention – however feasible it may seem.

This dearth of data has yielded a call for more serious research employing a variety of assessment tools rather than relying on small-scale studies and anecdotal observations. The standards and objectives published by the Association of College and Research Libraries (ACRL) in 2000 and 2001 have provided a baseline against which researchers may measure their assessment data. As members of the library and information science community address this call to gather and analyze data, journals are the most likely venue for publication in a timely manner.

Importance of the study

This study looked specifically at those scholarly journals in order to determine the degree to which the topic of information literacy has been (and is being) addressed in the literature and connected to critical thinking. A bibliometric analysis seemed to provide the appropriate method to make this determination. This analysis was the natural precursor to a more detailed content analysis of the journal literature.

Purpose of the study/problem statement

The purpose of this study was to analyze trends in publication on the subject of information literacy using bibliometric tools in order to provide an understanding of how the topic has been and is being addressed. It revealed who has published, what educational levels they examined, whether there has been a change over time in how frequently the topic has been addressed, and how frequently information literacy has been tied in a major way to the Web and technology.

Research questions

Specific research questions addressed in this study included:

RQ1   Beginning in 2000, how have articles on this topic been distributed by time (yearly)?

RQ2   What proportion of the articles published on 'information literacy' and 'critical thinking' focus the topic on academic libraries at institutions of higher learning?

RQ3   With what frequency do these articles carry the terms 'Internet,' 'Web,' 'digital,' 'online,' or 'technology' in their titles?

RQ4   What are the demographics of authorship on this topic (gender, affiliation, solo author, or multiple authors)?

Limitations/delimitations

This study was limited to research and featured articles found in peer-reviewed journals within the following databases: *Library Literature & Information Science* (*Library Lit*) and *Library, Information Science & Technology Abstracts* (*LISTA*).

While a brief examination of the contents of *Educational Resources Information Center* (*ERIC*) on this subject also revealed relevant materials, the scope and duration of the present study could not support that database's inclusion in the current analysis.

In addition to these articles, published texts made available through the University of Southern Mississippi have been included in the literature review. This study examined only those works published in the English language.

Definitions

Bibliometrics: The use of mathematical and statistical methodology to study and identify patterns in the usage of materials and services within a library or to analyze the historical development of a specific body of literature, especially its authorship, publication, and use.'[3]

Critical thinking: In research and scholarship, the skill required to develop effective and efficient search strategies, assess the relevance and accuracy of information retrieved, evaluate the authority of the person(s) or organization responsible for producing information content, and analyze the assumptions, evidence, and logical arguments presented in relevant sources.[4]

Information literacy: Skill in finding the information one needs, including an understanding of how libraries are organized, familiarity with the resources they provide (including information formats and search tools), and knowledge of commonly used research techniques. The concept also includes the skills required to critically evaluate information content and employ it effectively.[5]

Assumptions

It has been assumed that the information provided by the *Library Lit* and *LISTA* databases was accurate and representative of the literature in the field, specifically that the databases have been properly indexed and are complete regarding authorship.

Literature review

A search of related literature on this subject reveals a shift over time in how the topic has been understood and how it has been addressed. In the 1970s and 1980s, the focus was on library 'search' skills and evaluation of the effectiveness of programs developed by schools and universities to teach those skills. The presentations from the 11th Annual Library Instruction Conference in 1981 reveal this focus from a variety of perspectives: media specialists, academic librarians, classroom teachers, university faculty, etc. Published as *Teaching Library Use Competence: Bridging the Gap from High School to College*, there should be no surprise that the presentations center on the translation and transition of library use and skills instruction from secondary school to the post-secondary environment.[6] It is clear from the pieces included in this volume that the information being sought by students was almost exclusively in print form and other than card catalogs and the *Readers' Guide*, the reference librarian was the most valued resource available.

Information literacy

With the arrival of the 1990s, the focus of the literature shifted away from just 'library skills' and became more concerned with information and technology. By the middle of the 1990s, personal computers had become commonplace and the Internet was becoming more familiar every day. This revolution led to the era being dubbed the 'Information Age' and library instruction with its expanded scope became 'information literacy.'

Although this new concept gelled in the 1990s, the term was introduced in 1974 and it was the 1989 publication of the *American Library Association Presidential Committee on Information Literacy: Final Report* that provided an authoritative definition of 'information literacy' (one that differs only slightly from the one offered above):

- Knowing when information is needed
- Identifying the information needed to address a given problem or issue
- Finding the information needed
- Evaluating the needed information
- Organizing the needed information, and
- Using the information effectively to address the problem or issue at hand.[7]

Patricia Breivik, in her 1998 work *Student Learning in the Information Age*, advanced the call for information literacy instruction in higher education. Breivik specifically advocated for what she termed 'resource-based' instruction, embedding literacy instruction as a research component in the context of non-library courses within the students' curriculum. This volume provides one of the earlier connections between information literacy and critical thinking – the latter being strongly tied to resource-based learning.[8] Barbara Stripling continued in this vein with her 1999 compilation, *Learning and Libraries in an Information Age: Principles and Practice*, but with more emphasis on instructional methodology, standards-based assessment, and curriculum development.[9] Barbara Dewey's 2001 compilation, *Library User Education: Powerful Learning, Powerful Partnerships*, follows Stripling's lead to some extent but shifts the focus from instruction in general to partnered instruction – combining information literacy instruction with specific course-matter and tailoring the content to meet the needs of various campus sects.[10]

The arrival of Donald Case's *Looking for Information: A Survey of Research on Information Seeking, Needs, and Behavior* in 2002 marks a shift away from observation and instruction toward data collection, research, and assessment.[11] Intended as a handbook for scholars, Case offers examples of methods for studying information behavior as well as providing a review of research from earlier years. Susie Andretta, on the other hand, selects individual case studies in her *Information Literacy: A Practitioner's Guide* (2005) to present data captured in different information literacy instructional settings. Andretta also provides comparisons of various national standards and models for information literacy in the English-speaking world.[12] Continuing this theme is Teresa Neely's *Information Literacy Assessment* (2006) in which she drives home the importance of standards and assessments, especially in light of accreditation requirements. Neely takes the Association of College and Research Libraries (ACRL) Information Literacy Competency Standards as her basis and offers examples of how these can be incorporated into assignments accompanied by performance indicators and outcomes that can be tied to each for evaluation.[13]

In addition to these books, journal literature of the past two years also provides examples of the newfound emphasis on research, data collection, and assessment. Among this literature, 'Diversity in the Information Seeking Behavior of the Virtual Scholar: Institutional Comparisons' (2007) seems to take a note from Case's handbook by using digital tools to examine the information behavior of students at four universities.[14] David Mill's 'Undergraduate Information Resource Choices' (2008) takes a snapshot of student research trends by employing a citation analysis of undergraduate bibliographies during one academic year at a liberal arts college.[15] Approaching the issue of information literacy instruction from another angle, Laura Saunders used a Delphi study approach when she examined the question of what was likely to come. As she presents in her 2009 article, 'The Future of Information Literacy in Academic Libraries,' accrediting organizations, policy-makers, and librarians realize that the components of information literacy involve a great deal more than library research skills. Her panel of librarians foresees growing collaboration with faculty as information literacy is contextualized and developed into a complex set of tools that can be translated into a variety of situations.[16]

Critical thinking

As seen above, critical thinking has been explicitly associated with information literacy for at least a decade. The ACRL Information Literacy Competency Standards established in 2000 reveal the significance of critical thinking to information literacy:

- The information literate student determines the nature and extent of information needed.
- The information literate student accesses needed information effectively and efficiently.
- The information literate student evaluates information and its sources critically and incorporates selected information into his or her knowledge base and value system.
- The information literate student, individually or as a member of a group, uses information effectively to accomplish a specific purpose.
- The information literate student understands the economic, legal, and social issues surrounding the use of information and accesses and uses information ethically and legally.[17]

The increasing role of critical thinking in information literacy has become apparent in the journal literature of the past two years. Amy VanScoy and Megan Oakleaf make a research-based argument for curriculum integration when teaching information literacy in their 'Evidence vs. Anecdote: Using Syllabi to Plan Curriculum-Integrated Information Literacy Instruction' (2008).[18] Curriculum integration is one form of contextualizing information literacy by meshing literacy components into other courses; contextualizing allows students to hone their critical thinking skills. Rao, Cameron, and Gaskin-Noel turn things around in their 2009 article by proposing that general education competencies be integrated into information literacy courses to provide a platform for assessing the competencies of critical thinking, critical reading, quantitative reasoning, and writing, as well as information literacy.[19] Anthony Stamatoplos' recent article argues for yet another model, one addressing independent research (non-curricular) by students and recommending proactive librarian involvement with student-researchers in a mentoring role.[20]

A special issue of *College & Undergraduate Libraries* in 2008 presents a wealth of literature on the subject of critical thinking in the context of information literacy and serves to further demonstrate the attention this subtopic is receiving.[21] This double issue begins with a bibliographical review of the subject looking back to 1986.[22] Following this, Maryellen Allen's piece advances the case for the constructivist method as best for honing critical thinking skills, specifically in an online forum.[23] Another article co-written by four professors from Gonzaga University offers insight into how they have interlaced three courses from different disciplines to leverage instruction in each for a synergistic effect.[24] The article offered by Linda Taylor also argues for contextualization, presenting the case for adapting vocabulary used for information literacy instruction to terms specific to the field of application.[25] Other authors in this issue present their arguments for understanding how students think and how this needs to be incorporated into information literacy and critical thinking instruction.[26]

Bibliometric analyses

The only bibliometric analyses of information literacy discovered in the course of this study originate in Asia and do not address the topic from the perspective of critical thinking.[27] Edzan's 2007 study was limited to students in the field of computer science at one university and its analysis looked at papers written by those students rather than at the scholarly literature.[28] A 2006 piece by Tsay and Fang examines the scholarly literature on information literacy but from the perspective of type of document, country of publication, language of publication, and author productivity.[29] Nazim and Ahmad's 2007 work approaches the subject from the direction of scientific output looking at research trends from 1975 to 2000 to examine the evolution of various foci or subsets within the field that have developed over that period.[30]

The dearth of bibliometric analyses on information literacy in the West seems rather surprising when one considers how 'hot' the topic appears to have become, especially over the past decade. The research presented below, because of its limitations, shows only the tip of the iceberg. However, it reveals that there is a wealth of scholarship on this one subset of the topic – critical thinking – much less what appears to be available on the macro-level subject of information literacy as a whole.

Methodology

In order to assess the trends in journal scholarship on the topic of information literacy and critical thinking, data were gathered from the period since 2000 – the year that ACRL first published information literacy standards. To maintain the focus on librarianship and to provide parameters for the data set, this study looked only at those featured articles or research articles made available through the *Library Lit* and *LISTA* databases. The search parameters used in these databases were the terms 'information literacy AND critical thinking' published from 2000 to 2009 and limited to the English language. Brief communications, reviews, and editorials were eliminated from the analysis as was any article retrieved that did not actually address the topic.

The results were first sorted by year of publication and then whether the articles had the limited focus of the academic library or institution of higher learning (IHL). This reflects both the 'popularity' of the topic over time as well as the relevance of the scholarship to the IHL environment.

Titles were then reviewed for the inclusion of the terms 'technology,' 'digital,' 'Internet,' 'online,' and 'Web.' This revealed the degree to which the topic of 'information literacy and critical thinking' has been associated with these technological terms at the 'headline level.'

Finally, the retrieved articles were broken down on the basis of the demographics of authorship: gender, affiliation, and numbers of authors on a single article. Author gender data was categorized as 'male' or 'female' and gender ratios were examined overall as well as for each bracket of multiple authorship. Author affiliation was based on the organization type with which the author was affiliated at the time of publication, where this information was present in the article or associated with its abstract. Categories included 'IHL,' 'other education,' and 'government.' 'IHL' included all authors associated with colleges or universities whether librarians, researchers, instructors, or graduate students. 'Other education' encompassed authors in the field of education at the primary or secondary level, whereas, 'government' included authors affiliated with any non-school government entity.

Results

Using the methodology described above, 57 articles were found to meet the criteria (after duplicates were removed). The data extracted from these articles were compiled into an Excel spreadsheet and analyzed.

RQ1 Beginning in 2000, how have articles on this topic been distributed by time (yearly)?

The 57 articles yielded by this search were sorted by year of publication (see Figure A4.1). The first five years of the ten years examined produced only seven articles: none in 2002 or 2003, one in 2000, two in 2004, and four in 2001. From that mid-point forward (2005–09), publication rose overall but was unevenly distributed. Six articles were published in 2009, seven in 2005 and 2007, ten in 2006, and twenty in 2008.

Figure A4.1 Frequency of information literacy-critical thinking articles published by year

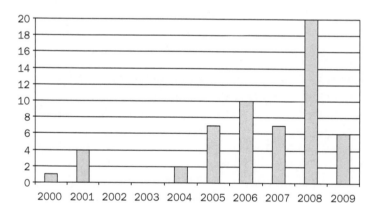

RQ2 What proportion of the articles published on 'information literacy' and 'critical thinking' focus the topic on academic libraries at institutions of higher learning?

Of the articles examined, 41 (72 percent) focused on information literacy and critical thinking in the context of institutions of higher learning and their associated libraries. The other 16 (28 percent) took a more generalist approach, examined the topic in a primary or secondary school context, or drilled down to one specific subtopic not tied to an IHL.

RQ3 With what frequency do these articles carry the terms 'Internet,' 'Web,' 'digital,' 'online,' or 'technology' in their titles?

Only six (10.5 percent) of the 57 articles included Internet or technological terms in their titles. Included in this number were those that referenced Web 2.0 and online courses.

RQ4 What are the demographics of authorship on this topic (gender, affiliation, solo author, or multiple authors)?

A total of 102 authors contributed to these 57 articles, with a gender distribution of 28 (27.5 percent) male authors and 74 (72.5 percent) female authors. As noted above, 16 of the 57 articles approached the topic from other than an IHL focus, yet only two of the 102 authors had an affiliation outside of the IHL arena – one government-affiliated and the other secondary school-affiliated.

While the majority of articles were written by more than one author, 26 (45.6 percent) were penned by solo authors. A decreasing trend appears as the numbers of authors increases: 19 articles had two authors, ten had three, and two articles had four authors. As seen in Table A4.1 and Figure A4.2, the trend of majority female authorship remains, regardless of the number of authors.

Table A4.1 Author quantity and gender distribution

# of authors for an article	# of articles with this many authors	%		Male	%	Female	%
1	26	45.6		10	38.5	16	61.5
2	19	33.3		8	21.0	30	79.0
3	10	17.5		7	23.3	23	76.7
4	2	3.5		3	37.5	5	62.5

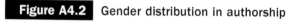

Figure A4.2 Gender distribution in authorship

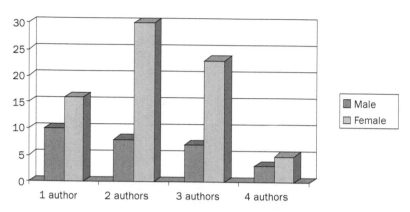

Discussion

The analysis of publication of articles by year between 2000 and 2009 indicates a sharp increase in the latter half of the decade. Although the overall quantity of articles was much greater in the latter five years than in the first five, 2008 may have been something of an anomaly. The topic-specific double issue of *College & Undergraduate Libraries* produced 11 of the 20 articles tabulated for 2008. It seems that short of such a themed publication, the general trend in the past five years has been six to ten articles per year.

The fact that 98 percent of the authors of these articles were affiliated with institutions of higher learning – even though their articles may not have addressed the topic with an IHL-focus – indicates that instructors, librarians, and researchers at IHL have taken the subject as their own. That over a quarter of the articles examined the subject with a non-IHL focus suggests that the authors are not restricting themselves to their own field when delving into the topic.

The gender distribution among the authors, weighted heavily towards females, may indicate that women now dominate the field. However, it could also suggest that women comprise the majority of the group of newcomers at institutions of higher learning, where publication is tied to tenure – young faculty are thus motivated to write. The data do not offer any clear insight into this question.

Suggestions for further study

This study explored the convergence of information literacy and critical thinking in scholarly literature but was limited in several directions. It looked at only a ten-year time window, examined only two databases, and reviewed only the surface layer of authorship data. A more complete picture of the scholarship on this topic may be possible if the time span under examination were expanded back to 1974, when the term 'information literacy' was first coined. Even if the time frame is kept compact, if more databases were included in the analysis there would likely be a larger body of material available for examination. Also, more in-depth analysis is possible regarding authorship, particularly from the direction of the role each of these IHL-affiliated authors has at their institution. This study presents only the first layer of analysis possible on this subject; there is a wealth of research to be done before the picture is complete.

Note: Data for this study are available in Excel format at: *http://spreadsheets.google.com/ccc?key=0AkzT2toPNJEZdFFIeVBvczly cFdGc1ZJRERDemNsSlE&hl=en*

Notes

1. David V. Loertscher and Blanche Woolls, *Information Literacy: A Review of the Research* (Salt Lake City, UT: Hi Willow Research and Publishing, 2002), 1n4.
2. Loertscher and Woolls, *Information Literacy*, 1n3.
3. Joan M. Reitz, *Dictionary for Library and Information Science* (Westport, CT: Libraries Unlimited, 2004), 73.
4. Reitz, *Dictionary*, 192.
5. Reitz, *Dictionary*, 356–7.
6. Carolyn A. Kirkendall (ed.), *Teaching Library Use Competence: Bridging the Gap from High School to College* (Ann Arbor, MI: Pierian Press, 1982).
7. American Library Association, *ALA Presidential Committee on Information Literacy: Final Report* (Chicago: ALA, 1989), 7, as cited in: Patricia Senn Breivik, *Student Learning in the Information Age* (Phoenix, AZ: Oryx Press, 1998), 3n4.
8. Breivik, *Student Learning*, 28.
9. Barbara Stripling (ed.), *Learning and Libraries in an Information Age: Principles and Practice* (Englewood, CO: Libraries Unlimited, 1999).
10. Barbara I. Dewey (ed.), *Library User Education: Powerful Learning, Powerful Partnerships* (Lanham, MD: Scarecrow Press, 2001).

11. Donald O. Case, *Looking for Information: A Survey of Research on Information Seeking, Needs, and Behavior* (San Diego, CA: Academic Press, 2002).

12. Susie Andretta, *Information Literacy: A Practitioner's Guide* (Oxford: Chandos, 2005).

13. Teresa Y. Neely, *Information Literacy Assessment: Standards-Based Tools and Assignments* (Chicago: ALA, 2006).

14. David Nicholas, Paul Huntington, and Hamid R. Jamali, 'Diversity in the information seeking behavior of the virtual scholar: institutional comparisons,' *Journal of Academic Librarianship*, 33, no. 6 (December 2007): 629–38. A similar study went beyond this 'which' analysis and investigated 'why' students engage in particular information behavior: Kyung-Sun Kim and Sei-Ching Joanna Sin, 'Perception and selection of information sources by undergraduate students: effects of avoidant style, confidence, and personal control in problem solving,' *Journal of Academic Librarianship*, 33, no. 6 (December 2007): 655–65.

15. David H. Mill, 'Undergraduate information resource choices,' *College & Research Libraries*, 69, no. 4 (July 2008): 342–55.

16. Laura Saunders, 'The future of information literacy in academic libraries: a Delphi study,' *portal: Libraries and the Academy*, 9, no. 1 (January 2009): 99–114.

17. Teresa Y. Neely, *Information Literacy Assessment: Standards-Based Tools and Assignments* (Chicago: ALA, 2006), 7n1.

18. Amy VanScoy and Megan J. Oakleaf, 'Evidence vs. anecdote: using syllabi to plan curriculum-integrated information literacy instruction,' *College & Research Libraries*, 69, no. 6 (November 2008): 566–75.

19. Srivalli Rao, Agnes Cameron, and Susan Gaskin-Noel, 'Embedding general education competencies into an online information literacy course,' *Journal of Library Administration*, 49, no. 1 (2009): 59–73.

20. Anthony Stamatoplos, 'The role of academic libraries in mentored undergraduate research: a model of engagement in the academic community,' *College & Research Libraries*, 70, no. 3 (May 2009): 235–49.

21. This issue was also later published as: John Spencer and Christopher Millson-Matula (eds), *Critical Thinking within the Library Program* (New York: Routledge, 2009).

22. Erin L. Ellis and Kara M. Whatley, 'The evolution of critical thinking skills in library instruction: a selected and annotated bibliography and review of selected programs,' *College & Undergraduate Libraries*, 15, no. 1/2 (2008): 5–20.

23. Maryellen Allen, 'Promoting critical thinking skills in online information literacy instruction using a constructivist approach,' *College & Undergraduate Libraries*, 15, no. 1/2 (2008): 21–38.

24. Mark Alfino, Michele Pajer, Linda Pierce, and Kelly O'Brien Jenks, 'Advancing critical thinking and information literacy skills in first-year college students,' *College & Undergraduate Libraries*, 15, no. 1/2 (2008): 81–98.

25. Linda Heichman Taylor, 'Information literacy in subject-specific vocabularies: a path to critical thinking,' *College & Undergraduate Libraries*, 15, no. 1/2 (2008): 141–58.

26. Pamela Hayes-Bohanan and Elizabeth Spievak, 'You can lead students to sources, but can you make them think?' *College & Undergraduate Libraries*, 15, no. 1/2 (2008): 173–210; and Corey M. Johnson, Elizabeth Blakesley Lindsay, and Scott Walter, 'Learning more about how they think: information literacy instruction in a campus-wide critical thinking project,' *College & Undergraduate Libraries*, 15, no. 1/2 (2008): 231–54.

27. The researcher does not include David Mill's citation analysis (addressed above) in this assessment because of Mills' generalized groupings of sources and lack of specificity.

28. N.N. Edzan, 'Tracing information literacy of computer science undergraduates: a content analysis of students' academic exercise,' *Malaysian Journal of Library & Information Science*, 12, no. 1 (July 2007): 97–109.

29. Ming-Yueh Tsay and Bih-Ling Fang, 'A bibliometric analysis on the literature of information literacy,' *Journal of Educational Media & Library Sciences*, 44, no. 2 (Winter 2006): 133–52.

30. Mohamed Nazim and Moin Ahmad, 'Research trends in information literacy: a bibliometric study,' *SRELS Journal of Information Management*, 44, no. 1 (March 2007): 53–62.

Bibliography

Alfino, Mark, Michele Pajer, Linda Pierce, and Kelly O'Brien Jenks (2008) 'Advancing critical thinking and information literacy skills in first-year college students,' *College & Undergraduate Libraries*, 15(1/2): 81–98.

Allen, Maryellen (2008) 'Promoting critical thinking skills in online information literacy instruction using a constructivist approach,' *College & Undergraduate Libraries*, 15(1/2): 21–38.

Andretta, Susie (2005) *Information Literacy: A Practitioner's Guide*. Oxford: Chandos.

Breivik, Patricia Senn (1998) *Student Learning in the Information Age*. Phoenix, AZ: Oryx Press.

Case, Donald O. (2002) *Looking for Information: A Survey of Research on Information Seeking, Needs, and Behavior*. San Diego, CA: Academic Press.

Dewey, Barbara I. (ed.) (2001) *Library User Education: Powerful Learning, Powerful Partnerships*. Lanham, MD: Scarecrow Press.

Edzan, N.N. (2007) 'Tracing information literacy of computer science undergraduates: a content analysis of students' academic exercise,' *Malaysian Journal of Library & Information Science*, 12(1): 97–109.

Ellis, Erin L. and Kara M. Whatley (2008) 'The evolution of critical thinking skills in library instruction: a selected and annotated bibliography and review of selected programs,' *College & Undergraduate Libraries*, 15(1/2): 5–20.

Hayes-Bohanan, Pamela and Elizabeth Spievak (2008) 'You can lead students to sources, but can you make them think?' *College & Undergraduate Libraries*, 15(1/2): 173–210.

Johnson, Corey M., Elizabeth Blakesley Lindsay, and Scott Walter (2008) 'Learning more about how they think: information literacy instruction in a campus-wide critical thinking project,' *College & Undergraduate Libraries*, 15(1/2): 231–54.

Kim, Kyung-Sun, and Sei-Ching Joanna Sin (2007) 'Perception and selection of information sources by undergraduate students: effects of avoidant style, confidence, and personal control in problem solving,' *Journal of Academic Librarianship*, 33(6): 655–65.

Kirkendall, Carolyn A. (ed.) (1982) *Teaching Library Use Competence: Bridging the Gap from High School to College*. Ann Arbor, MI: Pierian Press.

Loertscher, David V. and Blanche Woolls (2002) *Information Literacy: A Review of the Research*. Salt Lake City, UT: Hi Willow Research and Publishing.

Mill, David H. (2008) 'Undergraduate information resource choices,' *College & Research Libraries*, 69(4): 342–55.

Nazim, Mohamed and Moin Ahmad (2007) 'Research trends in information literacy: a bibliometric study,' *SRELS Journal of Information Management*, 44(1): 53–62.

Neely, Teresa Y. (2006) *Information Literacy Assessment: Standards-Based Tools and Assignments*. Chicago: ALA.

Nicholas, David, Paul Huntington, and Hamid R. Jamali (2007) 'Diversity in the information seeking behavior of the virtual scholar: institutional comparisons,' *Journal of Academic Librarianship*, 33(6): 629–38.

Rao, Srivalli, Agnes Cameron, and Susan Gaskin-Noel (2009) 'Embedding general education competencies into an online information literacy course,' *Journal of Library Administration*, 49(1): 59–73.

Reitz, Joan M. (2004) *Dictionary for Library and Information Science*. Westport, CT: Libraries Unlimited.

Saunders, Laura (2009) 'The future of information literacy in academic libraries: a Delphi study,' *portal: Libraries and the Academy*, 9(1): 99–114.

Stamatoplos, Anthony (2009) 'The role of academic libraries in mentored undergraduate research: a model of engagement in the academic community,' *College & Research Libraries*, 70(3): 235–49.

Stripling, Barbara K. (ed.) (1999) *Learning and Libraries in an Information Age: Principles and Practice.* Englewood, CO: Libraries Unlimited.

Taylor, Linda Heichman (2008) 'Information literacy in subject-specific vocabularies: a path to critical thinking,' *College & Undergraduate Libraries*, 15(1/2): 141–58.

Tsay, Ming-Yueh and Bih-Ling Fang (2006) 'A bibliometric analysis on the literature of information literacy,' *Journal of Educational Media & Library Sciences*, 44(2): 133–52.

VanScoy, Amy and Megan J. Oakleaf (2008) 'Evidence vs. anecdote: using syllabi to plan curriculum-integrated information literacy instruction,' *College & Research Libraries*, 69(6): 566–75.

Index